Our Encounters with Suicide

Edited by

Alec Grant, Judith Haire,
Fran Biley and Brendan Stone

PCCS BOOKS
Ross-on-Wye

First published 2013

PCCS BOOKS Ltd.
2 Cropper Row
Alton Road
Ross-on-Wye
Herefordshire
HR9 5LA
UK
Tel +44 (0)1989 763 900
www.pccs-books.co.uk

Our Encounters with Suicide

A CIP catalogue record for this book is available from the British Library

ISBN 978 1 906254 62 9

Front cover image: '–The Life Well Lived' by McLoughlin, 2012. Painting in a private collection.
Cover designed in the UK by Old Dog Graphics
Typeset in the UK by The Old Dog's Missus
Printed by 4edge Ltd, Hockley, Essex, UK

MIX
Paper from
responsible sources
FSC
www.fsc.org
FSC® C020822

Contents

Surviving suicide

Defending suicide

Acknowledgements

We wish to thank the following people and organisations, without whom this book would not have been possible:

- Heather Allan, Pete Sanders and their colleagues at PCCS Books. Writing for PCCS Books is always pleasurable because of the warm and professional support the staff unstintingly provide.

- All the contributing authors in this text, whose courage, tenacity, suffering and experiential wisdom are displayed in its pages.

- Our friend and colleague, the late Dr Francis C. Biley, who sadly died in November 2012. It had been Fran and Alec's idea to publish the first collection of 'experts by experience' narratives in 2011, and *Our Encounters with Madness* (PCCS Books) brought together largely unmediated mental health user, carer and survivor narratives from both sides of the Atlantic. Following its publication, Fran then wanted to develop a series of *Encounters* books. *Our Encounters with Suicide* and *Our Encounters with Self-Harm* were the two volumes in progress at the time he passed away. We would not have been able to publish *Our Encounters with Suicide* without Fran and his initial ideas and creative input. His enthusiasm and dedication were inspiring and he is greatly missed.

All royalties from the sale of this book will go to the Maytree Sanctuary for the Suicidal.

Dedications

Alec Grant
For my mother, Margaret Cameron Garden, 1914–1974,
and for my friend and esteemed co-researcher/writer, Fran Biley, 1958–2012

Judith Haire
For Ken, Maud, Jack

Fran Biley
To Anna, MJ, and James

Brendan Stone
Remembering Peggy, my mother

Forewords

Professor Gillian Bendelow and Dr Katherine Johnson

Professor Gillian Bendelow

The French sociologists Baudelot and Establet claim in their Durkheimian social history *Suicide: The Hidden Side of Modernity* that 'It isn't society that sheds light on suicide, but rather suicide that sheds light on society' (2008, p. 7). Their estimates that at the very least one in six people will be directly affected by suicide across North America and Northern Europe support the need to acknowledge its degree of visibility in our daily lives, as intrinsically part of what it means to be human, rather than rendering suicide as a highly individual pathological act and statistical exception. It is a somewhat daunting privilege to be asked to write a foreword to this brave and extraordinary book which uses personal narratives from a wide range of perspectives and experiences to illuminate and bring to life, as the introduction describes, the 'impersonal statistics'.

Arranged through five themes, Witnessing Suicide' Living in the Wake of Suicide, Thinking Suicide, Surviving Suicide and Defending Suicide, we are given insight into the complexity and multilayered facets of the experience across the spectrum of emotion from the darkest depths to the shimmers of hope and resilience. For some it is a process of living with endless struggle, for others a sense of survival. We are exposed to the difficult emotions of those dealing with the aftermath, or the ever-present possibility of losing loved ones, spanning shame, anger, guilt, resentment as well as pain and loss. The controversial question of the relationship between mental health and suicide is addressed from all angles and there is no easy answer or straightforward correlation. For some it may be a logical response to an 'unliveable' life, while for others appropriate therapeutic interventions have been life-saving.

Emotions are the mechanism linking mind, body and society, and the lens by which we process our being-in-the-world. We all experience emotional difficulties, whether or not we are prepared to admit it, and seeing our mental health along a spectrum where some may need help or intervention more than others is surely enlightening and desirable. In this way, understanding ourselves in terms of *emotional health* rather than mental illness is less stigmatising, exemplified in these mature and reflexive narratives. This book is accessible for every imaginable audience, and should be required reading for everyone entering the caring/ health professions. The stories vividly elicit the need to break possibly the ultimate societal 'taboo' around suicide and it seems axiomatic that the development of our emotional literacy in this way will ultimately equip us with a more communicative, empathetic and open society, which has far-reaching collective, as well as individual, implications.

Reference

Baudelot, C & Establet, R (2008) *Suicide: The hidden side of modernity.* Cambridge: Polity Press.

Gillian Bendelow

Before entering higher education as a mature student, Gillian Bendelow worked in London's East End as a ward sister and community psychiatric nurse. Between 1990 and 1995, she was a founder member of the Social Science Research Unit, University of London, where she completed her doctoral research in 1992 on the sociology of pain, under the supervision of Professor Ann Oakley, and with the help of an ESRC studentship award. From 1995 to 2003, she worked at the University of Warwick as a Lecturer in the Department of Social Policy and Social Work and as Senior Lecturer in the Department of Sociology. She was appointed as Reader to the Department of Sociology at the University of Sussex in 2003 and became Professor in 2006. Gillian has made significant research contributions to the fields of chronic pain and 'contested' illness conditions; mental health and emotional wellbeing; health promotion and lay concepts of health and illness. She is author of *Pain and Gender* (Pearson Education, 2000), *Health, Emotion and the Body* (Polity, 2009) and co-author of *The Lived Body* (Routledge, 1998) as well as many edited books and journal articles.

Dr Katherine Johnson

Suicidology, the scientific study of suicide, is a rich and complex area primarily concerned with better understanding and predicting suicidal risk, reducing the number of lives lost, and improving support for those bereaved by suicide. The field brings together researchers from psychiatry, medicine, psychology, sociology and social policy to tackle the issue of suicide on national and global scales. International support for this public health agenda has been recognised via the publication of new suicide prevention strategies in 2012 (in the US and the UK) and the goal of suicide reduction in the recently convened Global Movement for Mental Health. The UK Government has pledged a further £1.5 million to fund research for projects that will help reduce suicide in high-risk groups, improve media reporting on suicide, and support the bereaved.

In the pages that follow we find a timely reminder of what is at stake in contemporary suicide research. Crafted through the personal accounts of those touched by suicide, this deeply moving collection demonstrates that beyond the scope of suicide statistics, trends, risk factors and high-risk groups remains the importance of storytelling, and its central role in living a life that is marked by encounters with suicide. While our scientific methods might help us to model and predict suicidal risk within particular groups, they are unable to explain the multiple and highly individual narratives that underpin acts of suicide. Certainly, we see references to mental illness as well as defences of suicide as a reasonable response to unreasonable life situations. But, what is foremost amongst these narratives is a desire to make sense of suicide. What do the suicides of our friends, family members, lovers and our own struggles with suicidal thought and feelings communicate? What do they say about us as individuals, or the societies in which we live? It is in seeking to understand and to restructure our lives after an encounter with suicide that communication and storytelling have crucial roles.

Any bereavement, but particularly one through such sudden means, can launch us into a liminal state. Here our sense-making formulas are insufficient for managing the complex emotions a death triggers: feelings of guilt, shame, anger, regret, coupled sometimes with relief. Slowly we must reorientate ourselves to the world, incorporating the suicide into our own narrative, our own history, and our own being. Perhaps this is why those who have encountered suicide are themselves considered as a high-risk group – to have known suicide and accepted it may increase the likelihood of seeing suicide as a reasonable response to unliveable conditions. Yet, feeling suicidal, which Edwin Shneidman (1993) so eloquently describes as 'psychache', is also associated with acute isolation. It is in this context that dialogues about the pain of suicide, stories of its impact, feelings of loss, and narratives of resolution and forgiveness have the potential to resonate and connect us to others.

The light touch editorial approach taken in this book provides us with this opportunity. The editors have successfully shaped the chapters thematically, enabling the authors to speak to their truth, in an open and accessible format that extends an invitation to audiences looking for personal and professional answers to the questions suicide generates. And in these connections we are offered many things: understanding, support, recognition, and ultimately the possibility of a different ending.

Reference
Shneidman, E (1993) *Suicide as Psychache: A clinical approach to self-destructive behavior*. London: J. Aronson.

Katherine Johnson
Katherine Johnson is Principal Lecturer in the School of Applied Social Science, University of Brighton. Her research is located in the sub-disciplines of critical and community psychology with a specific focus on gender, sexuality and mental health. In recent years she has worked with the mental health charity MindOut on improving our understanding of suicidal distress amongst LGBT people, producing research that has informed suicide prevention policy. She is co-author of *Community Psychology and the Socio-economics of Mental Distress* (Palgrave Macmillan, 2012) and the single-authored book *Sexuality and the Psychosocial Subject* (Polity) which will be published in 2014.

Introduction

Alec Grant, Judith Haire and Brendan Stone

Stories of suicide might be reasonably placed under the rubric of 'forbidden narratives' (Church, 1995). Forbidden narratives disrupt society's tacitly held normative assumptions and practices – those which are accepted as normal, usual, predictable and reasonable, and enshrined and policed in policy and related texts – by conveying human experiences which are too unruly to fit with those assumptions and practices. The personal narrative rather than the impersonal statistic breaks the dehumanising taboo of suicide. To borrow a metaphor from Schon (1987), saying the unsayable may help shift those who draw on clear-cut, dismissive and prejudicial views about suicide from the high hard ground of certainty more towards the murky swamplands of not knowing. Further, Richardson (1997) reminds us of the positive moral function of collecting narratives of hitherto difficult, unspoken and private topics in helping rehabilitate them from neglected and isolating margins to supportive communities of storytelling and sharing. We learn about ourselves and each other from the stories we tell, and the stories told about us (Grant, 2011a; Grant & Zeeman, 2012). They provide us with rich templates for living and dying, and for making sometimes more acceptable sense of the past, present and future.

The aims of this book

Our overall aim in this book is that the frank accounts contained within it will be helpful for people who may have had similar encounters, or may be harbouring future suicidal intentions. We hope that, just as many of the writers found crafting their stories helpful, sometimes therapeutic, readers can use the stories in the book to make better sense of their own experiences and make better quality future decisions about their lives. We also hope that the book will facilitate a better understanding of the experiences of others generally, and of close family or friends who committed suicide.

A further wish is that those involved in working with people who contemplate, plan, execute and survive suicide will benefit from reading this book. Its pages will convey how sensitive professional and voluntary interventions and support can have a healing effect. Conversely, readers will see accounts of unwitting and sometimes deliberate insensitivity, defensiveness, neglect and abuse from professional services and workers within those services. All of this can compound the pain and confusion of people already unbearably mired in human distress. Professional and voluntary workers in mental health and other related services need to understand the differences between *knowing about* suicide from diagnostic or psychopathological texts and *knowing what it's like* to be suicidal. *Knowing about* may be useful for engaging with examination assignments. *Knowing what it's like* is essential for engaging with people.

The organisation of the book

The collection of suicide narratives constituting this book are written by contributors from both sides of the Atlantic. They are grouped as chapters within five themes, which appear in the book in the following sequence: Witnessing Suicide; Living in the Wake of Suicide, Thinking Suicide, Surviving Suicide, and Defending Suicide. In line with the first book in this series (Grant, Biley & Walker, 2011), we wish to provide a minimum of narrative analysis. However, this and the final chapter undeniably provide an analytic frame for the contributors' stories, as does the way they have been ordered as groups of chapters in the book. That said, the thematic groupings are intended mainly for the convenience and orientation of the reader in accessing chapters cohering around a common topic. Further, these chapters stand on their own merits and each has been proofread with a 'light touch' only. We have tried to preserve the integrity of the variety of idiosyncrasy of writing styles, including retaining North American spellings and spelling practices related to local cultures. Minor grammatical and punctuation changes were made only when absolutely necessary to enhance the readability and impact of contributors' work.

Some contributing authors have agreed to provide a list of bullet points at the end of their chapters. These indicate what has been learned from their experiences, and invite discussion, including around how things might have been handled differently and more effectively and sensitively by those others – family, friends and statutory service workers – involved in the event. For those authors who did not wish to provide such lists, this information is arguably implicit in their writing.

The chapters

Witnessing suicide

The only chapter in the *Witnessing Suicide* theme is 'Violent Impact' by Karl Davis. After conveying the first-hand experience of the suicide of a woman who threw herself in front of the train he was driving, Karl describes his experiences mediated by a long period of diagnosed post-traumatic difficulties. These included the tensions between his personal problems and the need to retain professionalism. He narrates his eventual connection with the family of the deceased, and how the helpful support he received from fellow train drivers was undermined by employers who regarded him as 'swinging the lead' and inadequate responses and support from the British National Health Service.

Living in the wake of suicide

The first two chapters in the theme *Living in the Wake of Suicide* are written by Pamela Kirk and Philippa Brook, mother and daughter respectively, about the suicide of their husband/father and son/brother. These chapters introduce a common broad theme that runs throughout the book: the effort to find meaning after, and sometimes before and during, the event of a family member, friend or colleague taking, or attempting to take, their own lives.

In 'A Lesson Learned All Too Well, Perhaps?' Stacey Autote writes about her family's transgenerational suicidal tendencies, modelling and suicide rehearsal conversations, and her brother's eventual suicide. Cath Walsh describes the loss of her sister in the next chapter, in an apparent attempt to try to make sense of her suicide a long time before the event. She writes about how her sister, as a negative role model for her, resisted marching to the same beat as everyone else in the pursuit of her fierce individual style. Following this, Catherine Carley writes about her mother's suicide from drowning. She interprets her mother taking her own life in terms of the external force of illness rather than personal choice.

In 'Gone but Not Forgotten', Georgina Smith poses a fairly common question related to personal meaning-making following the suicide of her boyfriend, who jumped from a multistorey car park: will I be able to move on? In the chapter following, Alex raises questions around the significance and status of suicide notes. Following his mother's failed suicide attempt, he was left with the issue of not knowing what to do with her notes, related to thorny questions around their significance and who should own them.

In 'Suicidal Wisdom', Jayne Stewart describes the suicide of her brother as a moral act, in a history of familial sexual abuse. Jayne describes her brother's suicide as facilitating the necessary exposure of a number of family secrets. The suicide of her uncle in the context of a close but troubled family left Karen McDonald with mixed troubling emotions which impacted the meaning of the event for her. In her chapter she describes her anger with the media, self-blame and doubts about her suitability for a career in mental health nursing. The tone of her story to some extent resonates with the next chapter, Abigal Muchecheti's 'Living on the Edge'. Abigal describes her feelings of uselessness, guilt and self-blame over the death of her cousin, for not detecting the signs of her intention to take her own life, asserting that she *should* have been able to do this.

In 'The Other Half', Jo Rhodes describes her husband's suicide in terms of his betrayal. After he took his own life, Jo found out the extent of his secret infidelities and huge debts that she was unaware of. The loss of her husband was subsequently compounded by a loss of trust and an absolute blaming of him for his actions in a context of treachery. In 'D', Gilly Graham writes about the suicide of a loved and respected work colleague. She describes classic grief stage experiences following this, including self-blame, disbelief, guilt and anger. She also attributes her colleague's decision to take his own life to the familiar concepts of choice, waste, selfishness, punishing and uncaring for those left behind. These concepts are taken up in the two chapters which bring the theme Living in the Wake of Suicide to a close: Neil Ritchie's 'A Lifetime Changed in a Moment' and Lost Soul's 'Self-Portrait'. Neil describes his sadness at not being able to provide help for the friend who took his own life, in a social context where most of his contacts regard suicide as a selfish act. Lost Soul writes about her belief that suicide is a complex act and not to be judged, despite the common cultural view of it as the coward's way out.

Thinking suicide

This theme brings together chapters which display suicide in multiple contexts, with, as would be expected, human distress at the forefront. In 'My Father's War', Sid Prise describes making a co-pact of suicide with his father but not carrying through on this. Sid concludes his chapter by expressing gladness about this and the hope that readers will also avoid taking this course. Ruth Kilner's 'Choosing to Be' raises issues about the contextual bases of suicide troubling and exceeding the narrow normative categories of public and professional understanding of the construct. In an account where she writes about suicide as a 'preventative cure', she describes how she makes a daily choice to live her life, which she experiences as liberating and empowering.

In the next chapter, Tessa Glaze writes about her planning suicide and the various ways of doing it in relation to the need to disappear and lose her sense of self. The context of this for Tessa is long-standing mental health problems around body image, social phobia and related depression. Depression similarly plagues Helen Harrop. In 'Semi-suicidal' she describes the 'too scared to live; too brave to die' dilemma she finds herself in. While she struggles to stay alive, she writes that she does not fear death, only the legacy for those left behind. Finally, in an untitled chapter, Naomi also links depression to suicidal ideation. However, she writes that, after attending the funeral of her friend's father who took his own life in 2011, she no longer sees suicide as an option for her.

Surviving suicide

The chapters in this theme raise questions and issues around stigma, shame and redemption and the societal tendency to judge suicide attempts in reductionist terms. The anonymous author of 'Suicide – My Story' describes the self-deprecating thoughts characteristic of depression. These included feeling not worthy enough to live, and feeling unacceptable compared with others. All hope gone, she made a serious attempt to kill herself by stepping off a London Underground platform in front of a train, but survived the attempt. Left with shame, she describes how she has benefited from appropriate help and now sees the value for herself and others of suicide survival.

In 'The Secrets of Suicide', Dawn Willis describes her own attitudes to suicide, and what she believes are society's, following her unsuccessful attempt to take her own life. She seems ambivalent in this regard, personally describing suicide as selfish, and identifying the societal view of it as an act born of cowardice and selfishness, while asserting that suicidal thoughts and actions are symptomatic of mental illness and should carry no shame. In the next chapter, Dolly Sen describes her suicide attempts in the context of abusive childhood experiences and psychosis. She writes about the failures of the statutory services to offer her effective help, and their sometimes abusive and homophobic interventions, as well as describing what she experienced as good, sensitive and effective healthcare.

Madame de Merteuil throws down the gauntlet in her chapter 'Phoenix to Ashes' in challenging those who are strangers to suicidal urges to understand beyond making such pejorative judgements around 'drama' and 'manipulation'. This raises the need for more complex and contextually sensitive understandings of suicide as a reasonable choice in the context of abusive life experiences, issues taken up in Felicity Stennett's chapter, 'The Day I Went to the Meadow'. The need to engage with negative societal judgements and judgements about self is further taken up by Kathryn, in 'Con Hearse'. She does this in relation to her damaged body and body image following her unsuccessful suicide attempt, and describes grappling with just what information to share in her work and private lives.

The theme of *Surviving Suicide* ends in a chapter by Michael Skinner called 'The Silence of Suicide' that begins with the lyrics to a song. This deals with Michael's losses of loved ones and friends to suicide. In addition, Michael points out the words also have meaning for him with regard to his own life struggles and surviving several suicide attempts.

Defending suicide

As they work their way through the book, readers may spot threads and sub-texts emerging which allude to a justification for suicide. As its name suggests, the two chapters in this last theme do this more explicitly. In 'In Defense of Suicide', Kathryn Rosenfeld provides a politico-affective pro-suicide argument, arguing for its moral acceptability in the face of a life that, for many, is not all that it's cracked up to be. The final contributor chapter, by Chrissie Hinde, 'A Red Sadness: My Dad's Story', picks up on some of these issues in arguing for 'suicidal wisdom', which positions suicide as a sometimes reasonable choice in the face of unbearable or relentless suffering.

In the final chapter, Alec Grant draws out the importance of narrative sense-making around suicide on the basis of his own encounters with the phenomenon. Drawing on narrative principles and theory from the social and human sciences and the humanities, he discusses some issues around the place of metaphor in suicide sense-making, with a focus on the significance of the suicide note. He concludes that suicide narratives, told by 'experts by experience', always exceed formal attempts to categorise the phenomenon.

The book ends with brief biographies provided by most of the contributing authors, the reference section, and hopefully some helpful appendices.

WITNESSING SUICIDE

2

Violent impact

Karl Davis

My first exposure to suicide was in my professional role as a train driver. The date, time, ambient lighting conditions, and colour of the jacket that the lady was wearing as she ended her life right in front of me are burned forever into my memory. I had only been qualified to drive trains for a few months, but was confident in my ability to react to any emergency, given the exhaustive training I had received, and almost constant assessment and examination. Looking back on the whole incident now, some nine-and-a-half years later, I manage a wry smile at the dawning realisation of my naivety, and indeed the failure of the privatised railway system in adequately preparing me for the psychological trauma that was unleashed by the last act of a desperate and tragic woman.

October 13th, 2002 had provided me with a quiet and uneventful late shift. It was a lovely autumn night. I had just eaten, and was feeling quite content with my lot as I guided my train through the countryside under the fading light of the evening. Despite it being a Sunday, the train was actually fairly busy with people heading out to the clubs and pubs within various market towns across the region. Having completed another station stop, the conductor closed the doors and signalled to me it was time to leave. Releasing the train's brakes, I opened the throttle, and we pulled away from the platform. I concentrated my attention on the line ahead as my eyes readjusted to the dark, the lights of the town centre fading quickly behind us. Reaching 70 mph, I closed the train's throttle, maintaining our speed as we hurtled through farmland toward our next stop.

As we passed over a level crossing, the train passed a 'whistleboard' (a white, round sign with a black 'W' in the centre, which commands the driver of a train to sound the horn). As I did so, a figure in a blue jacket stepped into the path of the train, holding out her arms like a goalkeeper trying to block the path of an opponent.

As I sit here now typing this, I can still feel the sensation that ran through my upper body as my mind processed and then reacted to what was happening on the other side of the windscreen. I can only describe it as a mild electric shock, not painful, but very bizarre as it swept up my torso and along my arms. I lurched forward, grabbing for the brake controller and pushing it to 'emergency', slamming the train's brakes fully on as I groped for the radio and jabbed the emergency call button. The train's coupler slammed into her upper body, throwing her violently down the embankment with a sickening thud even before the brakes had fully applied themselves.

With hindsight, I feel almost as if the woman who committed suicide not only impacted with the front of the train, she bounced off me as well. I remember clearly the order, intent, and brevity of my communications with the signaller, the British Transport Police, and my company's control room, and the actions I took to make the train and the scene safe, but I still to this day do not recall feeling a single emotion until the train had lurched noisily to a standstill half a mile further along the line, and the signaller had told me to 'Take a moment to slow down and gather myself' before the police and response teams arrived.

In that sense, the training that I had received over the preceding year had been successful in erecting a protective shield around me in the immediate aftermath of the incident. I had immediately thrown myself into the task of protecting train and passengers, my mind filling itself with procedures, emergency drills and checklists to be completed. Revisiting the incident, the substantial memory for me was my acting in a seemingly disconnected manner emotionally speaking, and that left me racked with feelings of guilt for weeks afterwards.

I remember sitting back in the driving seat of the train, the line, train and passengers having been protected and the metaphorical dust beginning to settle. The first compulsion I felt, and subsequently repelled, was the need to grab my first aid kit and climb down from the train in an attempt to administer some sort of medical assistance. I felt responsible, and as such wanted to try and help the woman who had been hit by the train, my train! I felt like I wanted to bandage her up, to help her start to heal. Obviously there was not even the remote possibility that anyone could have survived such a violent and brutal impact, and it was this logical reasoning that I used to forcibly defeat the irrational voice in my head that would have directed me toward the door, sticking plasters in hand.

I recall vividly looking down at my hands as they shook violently and pursing my lips as my mouth ran dry. The conductor contacted me over the intercom and we passed operational details back and forth. He then busied himself with customer care, leaving me to await the arrival of the police and response teams in an eerie silence, my reflection staring back at me from the windscreen.

Even then, the full gravity of the trauma did not hit me. I calmly contacted my company's control centre, offering advice on the best route for the emergency relief driver to take in order to avoid having to step over the remains of the deceased, and re-contacted the conductor in order to offer assistance with arranging alternative arrangements for stranded passengers. He politely declined my offer, assuring me that it was all in hand.

As I spoke to him I heard some raised voices coming from outside. Peering out of the cab window, I saw a small group of teenagers, gathered by a crossing gate and understandably curious as to what was going on. One of them shouted across to me, 'Have you just killed someone mate?'

'I think it'd be best if you lot did one.' Grasping for an answer, this was the best I could come up with. The boy told me to 'Fuck off' and I spilled over with anger, launching a volley of abuse at the boy and his friends. I think the fury of my response surprised and probably frightened them a little and they promptly scattered.

'Sit down and relax,' said the conductor. I'd clean forgotten that I was holding the phone for the intercom in my hand! He had heard everything! Now, not only was I feeling guilty, angry, and helpless, I was also feeling embarrassed. Being a career railwayman with many years of experience under his belt, as well as having witnessed a multitude of fatalities and the like during his time, I think that he recognised that an ordered and calm reaction to the incident was, on my part, turning into shock. A few minutes later, he appeared at the cab door, hot tea in hand, armed with some bad jokes in a bid to break the tension.

The intensity of my response to those teenagers surprised me. I condemned myself for that, almost as much as I had done for the fatality itself, at least initially. They weren't involved, they weren't to blame. They were just kids acting like kids. I felt like a bully as well as a killer, yet at the same time I felt a duty to act in a calm and measured way towards my colleagues and to the passengers on the train. Shock was now giving way to an urge to get off the train and run until I ran out of breath. Not only did I feel guilty, and responsible as the driver of the train, I felt even more guilt at having to stifle the urge to run.

After what had seemed like an age, the first police officers were on the scene, diligently asking questions and noting down details, asking about my welfare and generally doing an excellent job in terms of processing the incident. Not long after, the emergency relief driver, along with a Driver Standards Manager, arrived. I was relieved of my duty and train, and driven back to my depot to complete reports and post-incident interviews.

Having completed all of the initial paperwork, I was driven home and placed on sick leave pending a doctor's examination. Arriving home, I went straight up to bed, sliding under the covers and staring at the ceiling, the whole incident replaying in my mind on a constant repeat. By 2 a.m. I was sat at the top of the stairs, my mind still racing as I looked at the frosted glass of the front door, thinking about the police knocking on the door of my 'victim' and imagining how abjectly lost her family would feel. I was utterly numb.

Strangely, through all of this, I had not once felt the urge to cry. I was confused. I thought that crying would be the natural thing to do. The fact that I didn't want to made me feel as if I was doing something wrong. Since then, I have come to the realisation that there is no 'right' way for anyone going through this to feel or to act. People are individuals. Just as people have different ways of driving, raising children, and styling their hair, they have their own, unique ways of dealing with trauma.

In the days that followed, I was very fortunate in that my family closed ranks around me and almost forced me to lean on them. This is something I found very hard to do, but with their persistence, and my growing fragility, I relented. At the time, I never recognised the value of supportive family. I have supportive friends, and I was inundated with concern from colleagues, managers, fellow union officials and acquaintances, but the fact that my family dropped what they were doing, and concentrated their efforts on helping me to 'pick myself up' made me feel strong enough to start trying to move on from the loop of that fateful night that seemed to endlessly repeat in my head.

Having been advised to consult my doctor, I spent a couple of days summoning up the courage to make an appointment. I felt as if I were some kind of fraud, as if I were not deserving of medical attention. I still felt incredibly guilty, responsible, and above all awkward about the fact that circumstance had played such a dreadful trick on me.

In the next day or two, the full gravity of the trauma I had felt seemed to finally crash down upon me. I couldn't sleep. I couldn't endure any darkness in my house. I wouldn't answer the phone or the door, and I couldn't face driving my car. I was rapidly careering downward, and I knew I had to arrest my sliding mentality when I was overcome by the irrational urge to shave my head. I had an almost burning need to rid myself of everything that had been on me, including my own hair, when the incident happened. I wanted to cleanse myself, and that compulsion began to worry me. Having tidied up my roughly shorn head, I sat in the kitchen, trying to level myself out. My body stiffened as I heard a loud knock at the door, but I forced myself to go and answer it. It was my best friend Mike, a fellow train driver. He looked at me in a mixture of concern, and shock, given my new haircut.

'You look like a fucking convict,' were his opening words, and I knew I had to take the first step and go and see my GP. Without uttering a further word he made us a cup of tea, and we started to talk things through, not like relatives, or concerned onlookers, or clinicians, but as train drivers. Speaking to my friend, who not only understood me, but also the demands and mind-set of our job, was a massive help. I felt unable to convey to my family how I was feeling. I was certain that they did not understand because they would never be in my place, somewhere only another driver would relate to being. Mike reassured me again and again that none of this was my fault, something I was aware of, despite my refusal to believe it. I felt safe discussing things with someone who knew what it was like to carry the safety of hundreds of people on your shoulders every day, someone who knew the culture of railways, and of train drivers. We are seen by others within our industry as 'cliquey' and 'protective of our own'. We carry a mutual concern for each other, and our colleagues' safety and wellbeing. The press label that sentiment as militancy, but to us it is about looking out for one another, and acting in the common good. When you qualify, you become a member of a professional family. This is something that makes me very proud to be a train driver, and it's never truer than in the case of a fatality, or other serious incident. In my hour of need, it was this collective shoulder that I craved.

Having given in to the nagging of my friend, and indeed my family, I built myself up to face my doctor, and duly went along to the health centre. Entering the consulting room, my hard-pressed GP barely looked up from his notes.

'How are you today?' he asked, still scribbling unintelligibly on a pad.

I explained why I had made the appointment, my heart beginning to beat faster as I expected him to throw down his pen and lecture me about the scarcity of NHS resources, or tell me not to be so ridiculous. He did neither. His first action was to reach into his drawer and produce a prescription pad. Still not looking at me, he scrawled something across the form and pushed it across the table. Picking it up, I managed to decipher the writing. The prescription was for Prozac. I sat there reading the script over and over, part mystified, part horrified. I was of the impression that only 'crazy' people took Prozac! I asked why the doctor had prescribed me Prozac, and he replied with a wave of the hand that it would assist my application for criminal injuries compensation.

'It's up to you whether you want to actually take them,' he said. 'Just make sure you get the tablets so it's recorded.'

I nodded blankly. I hadn't even considered the prospect of criminal injuries compensation! If I'm honest, it felt somewhat mercenary to be thinking in monetary terms after having witnessed the end of another person's life. I felt so angry at the casual tone in which I essentially had tablets thrown at me without any attempt to talk to me about what I was feeling, what I had suffered, how I was coping. I could feel my frustration bubbling up inside me, and was deliberately restraining myself, the memory of the teenagers gathered curiously at the scene still fresh in my mind.

'I've put you on the list for counselling too,' said the doctor. He produced another pad and wrote me a sick note. 'Six weeks,' he said, this time handing me the paper. Managing a smile, he wished me well and told me to come back if I had any problems or needed any help, before returning his attentions to his paperwork, a clear sign that our consultation was over.

Leaving the health centre, I felt no more reassured or equipped to effectively face what I was going through than I did in the initial moments following the incident. I felt as if I had been palmed off with a prescription and a sick note with nothing more in terms of healthcare intervention than a pat on the head and a promise that someone would contact me at some point in the future.

That evening, I took the Prozac the doctor had prescribed. After a few initial doses I felt unable to function. I felt as if I was wrapped in plastic, unable to communicate with those around me. I sat in a chair, staring absently into space. I fell asleep in an armchair and awoke 17 hours later, frightened and confused, my head throbbing. After the headache had subsided, I put the tablets in a drawer and later returned them to the pharmacy. Drugs most definitely were not the answer.

For the record, it took the NHS Counselling team for my locality more than SIX MONTHS to write to me and offer me an appointment. I am in a fortunate position, in that my union have negotiated agreements and provisions that provide access to private counselling at the company's expense. Whilst this is clearly a benevolent agreement, there is a financial imperative for the company to have their extensively trained, well-paid drivers back at work, driving trains, and generating revenue. Having spoken to my company's Employee Welfare Officer the following week, I was referred to a psychologist in Leeds, and an appointment was made for the following day.

I remember sitting in a very comfortable chair as this kindly man smiled, nodded, and furrowed his studious brow, almost in sequence as I finally began regaling him with the details of that awful night, and the alien experiences of the following few days, having sat staring out of the window for the first 20 minutes, unsure as to what was expected of me, and unsure as to what this man would make of what I had to say.

Words seemed to fail me at first, but I kept telling myself that it 'didn't matter what he thought of me', and that I'd 'probably never see him again'. Having convinced myself of that fact, I looked him in the eye, and despite feeling sick, started talking.

I told him how I couldn't sleep, how terrified the thought of driving my car made me feel, how I was struggling to eat or leave the house. I told him of my compulsion to shave my head, and how I was sure that, had I not forced myself to step back, I may have ended up putting all of my uniform, boots and equipment into bags and throwing them in the bin. I told him about how I could not handle large groups of people, or sudden and loud noises; how a union colleague spent the best part of three days persuading me to stay with him so I could attend a function in Newcastle, and how after I had disappeared half-way through the party, my friend found me crying on the fire escape because I felt so overwhelmed by the large throngs of people and the loud music. I told him about the bizarre and horrific dreams and night terrors that invaded what little sleep I was able to catch each night, and about the constant replays of the incident. I told him about the sound of the impact echoing in my mind, and how I had been affected in even the most intimate of ways, partially through guilt, and also because the sound and image of the incident never seemed to leave me, even for a second.

Laying my thoughts and emotions out for a complete stranger to analyse was intimidating, and in many ways humiliating. Overall though, it felt cathartic to finally speak freely about the pain and trauma I was feeling. Paradoxically, having spoken with my best friend, and fellow colleague, I now felt liberated to be sharing this burden with somebody with whom I had no personal or professional association whatsoever.

The psychologist engaged in a series of breathing exercises with me in a bid to minimise the physiological manifestation of the trauma, which we did over repeated sessions in addition to talking the incident through. We subsequently, after a few weeks, progressed to an exercise whereby I sat in front of an LED display and followed a moving dot with my eyes. As I did this, the psychologist asked me a number of questions about the incident, which I was able to recall in miniscule detail. He walked me through the incident in a bid to confront its gravity, and therefore negate its effect. Whilst I certainly was not completely recovered after the first session, I felt so much better. We repeated the exercises on another two occasions. Having confronted the incident 'head on' I felt as if it had lost much of its venom, thus making it more manageable. I felt able to 'put it to one side' for the first time in weeks.

As time passed, my anger, guilt and despair turned into a deep concern for the family of the deceased. Whereas I had wallowed in the thought of their suffering in the days immediately following the incident, I was now feeling real empathy for their pain. I was summoned to attend the coroner's inquest, where I was questioned extensively by HM Coroner under the intense and searching gaze of the deceased's son. Revisiting the incident was painful, especially so given the starkness of the medical evidence and police reports, and presence of the deceased's family.

At the end of the hearing I excused myself and headed for the toilets in order to gather my thoughts and wash my face. Wiping the cold water from my brow, I turned around to be confronted by the deceased's son. Unsure of what he wanted, I nervously eyed the door. Before I could speak he stepped forward, holding out his hand.

'I just wanted to apologise on behalf of my mother. She should never have put you through such an ordeal. I'm so sorry,' he said. I was dumbfounded. I took his hand and shook it, trying to reassure him that his ordeal was the greater. He left the room without replying to me. As he left, I felt so sorry for him and his family. The death of his mother would stay with me for the rest of my life. To this day I feel a bizarre connection with a perfect stranger who I never knew, and with whom I shared the most vulnerable time in her life. Where I feel connection, he feels abandonment, and where my wounds and pain would fade with time, his would never diminish. Nevertheless, I felt uplifted as I left the building. There was a time during my recovery where I would have been consumed with guilt at feeling such a positive emotion, but the excellent counselling I received, the unswerving support of my family, and understanding and empathy of my colleagues, and the astonishing display of humanity on the part of the deceased's son had conspired to make me feel strong enough to consider myself entitled to positive emotions.

It was seven-and-a-half months from the night where my train ended the life of the deceased to the time when I nervously drove a train again. In that time, in addition to everything I have written here, I was bullied by managers within my company, who repeatedly implied that I was 'swinging the lead'. I had my pay reduced by half with the company refusing to even meet me in order to discuss it. I came to really appreciate the importance of family support, as well as the priceless value of simply talking through the incident with my colleagues. The support of those who understand is such a precious commodity, and is just as vital as intervention from trained professionals.

I have found that the standard of treatment offered by some GPs is appalling, whilst others are excellent. I was immensely frustrated by the approach of my GP. In my experience, the NHS counselling services offered within my locality were simply unable to adequately meet the needs of patients in a timely fashion. I had resumed driving duties before I was contacted with the offer of an appointment.

Like I have mentioned previously, I was fortunate in that I was able to access private counselling. The majority of patients are not so lucky. As a passionate defender of the NHS and the public sector, the fact that I had to rely on the private sector to facilitate my recovery due to inadequacies in the public sector is something I still very much regret to this day.

I have found also that the training of management, and the awareness and ability of managers to deal with these incidents, varies massively. There seems to be a default opinion on the part of a sizeable number of managers that their workers are exploiting the system. In my experience, those who have gone through the trauma of dealing with suicide as part of their job should be utilised in training programmes in order to promote awareness and understanding, so managers can meet the human factors requirement more effectively, as well as simply being able to not come across to their traumatised staff as incompetent bullies. Health professionals also need to approach workers in these positions, bearing in mind that the person concerned has been thrown into this traumatic vortex by the actions of another, usually in a situation about which he or she knows nothing. The shock and guilt I felt made me act defensively toward healthcare professionals, and the attitude of my GP made me feel as if I had entered into some kind of queuing system whereby I was nothing more than an irritant who happened to have been assigned a number to be dealt with sequentially, irrespective of my needs, worries or fears.

I did apply for criminal injuries compensation. I was refused twice on the most spurious of grounds, the letter I received being unintelligible to all but the most fluent speaker of 'legalese'. Again, I count myself as fortunate in that my union instructed a barrister to lodge an appeal to a tribunal panel, who awarded me £1000 for my suffering and trauma. This took four long years to resolve. I felt as if my pain and trauma were being questioned by the State, and as such I was determined to make them admit that they were wrong.

Whilst the money was of secondary importance, the vindication of what I, my family, colleagues, and indeed the family of the deceased had been through was comforting, and offered me a small semblance of closure.

It was a full six years before I cried for the deceased, and for the trauma I had suffered. On the sixth anniversary I was overcome with emotion, holding court in my local and telling the barman to keep me stocked as I drank solidly from lunchtime until late evening. I stumbled out of the bar, mumbling and swaying, and walked until I reached the seafront, sitting for the next hour or so, sobbing as I sat cross-legged on the beach, fuzzy memories of the incident spinning around in my head.

Far from it being a regression, it did me the world of good. It finally released many of the demons that had been pent up inside of me, despite the counselling I had undergone, and the support I had enjoyed. I still think of the deceased often. My mood does darken somewhat in the days leading up to the anniversary, but that is only a healthy recognition of the gravity of what I endured. I have a drink to the deceased and make a toast to her family, and still marvel at the humanity displayed by her son.

Not only has my experience highlighted the failings of the system in so many areas; it has also highlighted the startling ability of people to show compassion, even in their darkest hour. In that way, I feel as connected to the memory of meeting the deceased's son, and the empathic spirit he showed, as I do to the part I played in the end of his mother's turbulent life.

LIVING IN THE WAKE OF SUICIDE

3

Pamela

Pamela Kirk

After the suicide of my husband and son ten years ago, I find that I still struggle with 'what if' and 'why' on a daily basis. In the beginning I felt sorry for them for what they had done; that they found themselves unable to go on for whatever reasons, which I now think will never be fully known or resolved.

People around me at the time expressed their opinion of what a good man my husband was and that they believed he was a considerate and kind-hearted person who would help anyone. Although these reflections were true regarding his character, I found that his actions had been most inconsiderate to the point of selfishness at leaving my daughter and me not only with the tragedy of one death, but to also take his own life and leave us to cope alone. This is an action I still find unforgivable. People also said that he was brave to do what he did, and to this day I cannot understand how anyone could think that. Surely it is braver to live.

I now see suicide as neither cowardly nor brave but an emotional imbalance in someone where the result is tragic regardless of whether the attempt is a success or a failure. For some time after the event it seemed that other people could freely talk about their feelings whilst I felt that if I was candid then I would be deemed as heartless and uncaring. There is also a taboo with regard to suicide that makes it difficult for me whenever I am asked how many children I have. It didn't seem to matter that my husband (no matter what the circumstances) should have been with me and my daughter so that we could all comfort each other over the death of our son.

With a history of drug addiction and a few failed suicide attempts I sometimes used to think that it was inevitable that my son might meet with a tragic end, but at the same time I thought each time he got better that he was recovering successfully and he could lead a normal life. Because of the emotional swings involved with his recovery then subsequent relapses whilst he was alive, I somehow managed to convince myself that although he had taken his own life, he never meant to do it, and never meant to hurt anyone. Because of this I also sometimes feel that of my two children I am glad that it is my daughter who is still with me and not my son, which leads to guilt. Again people around me still talk about what a great lad he was yet they never had to cope with the problems he caused due to his addiction.

It is very difficult to lose a child in any circumstances, but sometimes I feel like I spent so much of my life bringing him up, teaching him what he needed to live, only for him to choose to die. No one should outlive their children.

I found that most memories after this tragic event tended to be difficult and sad, but as time has gone on I am finding it easier and more beneficial to recall happier times.

Philippa

Philippa Brook

I'm alone,
Because I found you,
The way I never wanted to,
And I saw you,
But too late to see you go,
Too late to say goodbye.
Too soon I found you,
Knew what it was to lose you,
And I feel old.

I thought about what to put in this piece: from a detailed and graphic narrative of events, to a few hundred words of polished prose, but both of those alternatives are pointless. For purposes of identification I will say that the warm blanket of shock and tragedy is something I remember vividly, comforting like a lover. Sometimes I'd do anything to have it back. I still feel the physical pain of it sometimes. Funny that you expect the pain to be in your heart, but it's lower in your gut, as if you'd been stabbed. I also remember being angry that they'd left that way, because I knew straight away I couldn't follow. And at times I've really, really wanted to. For me (being bipolar in addition), suicide is a physical presence that I live with on a daily basis. At times it's as if it waits for me, and as long as it waits, I'll keep it waiting.

Above then is a poem I wrote upon finding the bodies of my father and brother in our home, a few days after they committed suicide. Below is something I posted on a forum for suicide survivors which has prompted messages of thanks for the hope in it. If you're suffering, I hope you take some comfort:

Regarding my own situation, there have been two suicides in my family. My brother took a drugs overdose, and when my father discovered him, he took an overdose of painkillers. I found them a few days later. My mother and I were living apart from them, so we don't know how much time had passed.

It's pure conjecture as to whether Paul was still alive when my dad found him. He may have been, but couldn't be resuscitated. There were signs of a resuscitation attempt. We do know that Paul died first. Again, we don't know how long my dad spent alone in the house before following him.

I hope that if there is ever another me out there, that you might find this, and feel a little less alone.

The most important things I can think to say, as concisely as I can, and in no particular order, are:

It's not your fault.

You're right; things will never be the same, but don't be afraid. It won't always be the same as it is now, either.

You are supposed to survive this. I say that because I am supposed to survive this. I have to.

You will learn how to live, literally, in a way that most people never have to think about. That's not a disadvantage.

Most people don't recognise happiness. You will. That's not a disadvantage either.

If your story is similar to mine, there's no point in denying that it's a large part of who we are. But it's not all of who we are. There were chapters before this, and there are chapters after it. Make them amazing. We are here to make each other happy.

Lastly, again it's really not your fault, and I can confidently say that, despite knowing nothing about you or those you have lost. That point is so important it seemed worthwhile putting it in there twice.

A lesson learned all too well, perhaps?

Stacey Autote

September 29, 2012 was the first anniversary of the death of my younger brother. Dead from suicide at 31 years old. He wasn't one of those suicides where at the service everyone stood around and said how shocked they were that this happened; more how shocked they were he lasted as long as he did. My brother suffered from severe bipolar depression, which was not properly treated or managed throughout his entire life.

Over the years my brother had tried to take his own life many times. I honestly don't remember the number of times we sat with him in the Emergency Room. I watched him sometimes drink the black charcoal mixture, sometimes it was given to him in a tube through his nose. It was used to make him throw up the pills and alcohol he had used to wash them down. Every time afterwards he was always the Charmer, Mr Smooth Talker. The psych doctor would come down and ask him what happened. He would say he overdid himself 'partying', and that it was purely an accident. The doctor would ask him if he was depressed at all or wanted to talk? My brother would tell the doctor that he was fine and that he wanted to go home, to his condo. He would go on about how his condo was a safe environment, with healthy foods that he liked to prepare himself. Within about six to eight hours, start to finish, we were dropping him off at his condo. Threats of him hurting himself were a fairly regular occurrence when he was younger. Around his mid-20s they stopped becoming threats and became something we as a family had to deal with quite a lot. Sometimes it was pills and alcohol, other times he would dart into traffic on a busy street. On one occasion my mom came home to find him sitting in the dark with a loaded shotgun between his legs. She called the police when he wouldn't give up the gun. He told the police, my mom didn't live in the best neighborhood and he didn't feel safe sitting outside alone. Even though my mom told the police about his many suicide attempts they walked away, doing nothing.

So many times we begged him to go into treatment, to try and get serious help. His paranoid state of mind made that impossible. He would see his primary care doctor after a suicide attempt, and the doctor would tell him how fast his system must metabolize medicine and alcohol because normal people would be dead with the doses he took! My brother would laugh and flash a smile. People would argue with my mom. Telling her it was all just a cry for attention. She should ignore him, or practice tough love. Making comments like: 'Let him run into the street and see what happens', 'People who are going to kill themselves don't talk about it', 'He knew that wasn't enough pills to really kill him!' or 'Tell him to do it already and leave you alone!' Even in his most manic rages, we tried to support him, and believe me that was not easy. One minute you could be his best friend, and the next minute he hated you with a fire of a million suns!! What made it worse was sometimes you didn't even know why he was hating you.

When I got the message that he was DEAD! That this time he had actually done it, I was in shock! He had made sure this time there no was coming back, no waking up!! He had done his research, devised a plan. Learned from a past failed attempt, corrected his mistakes and this time it worked. Maybe there is something to what people say about not talking about it, because he didn't this time. He just prepared a special noose he researched on the internet with a heavy duty extension cord, to insure the cord didn't snap, and I don't think I need to go into the rest of the details.

Now as I look back on his life, and mine, I wonder why he so desperately thought suicide was the answer to all his problems. I also suffer from severe depression and anxiety, but I am not bipolar. We experienced some similar traumatic childhood experiences. In my early teens to my late 20s I went through some incredibly hard times. So many days I laid in my bed unable to will myself to get up, unable to wash my hair, unable go to school or work, wishing with every bone in my body that I would go to sleep and not wake up. What did I do no matter what? Drag myself out of bed to take care of my incredibly sweet and loving two little dogs. They would look up at me with their tiny brown eyes, and wag their little tails. They needed me, I was responsible for them! I was like their mother. I couldn't let them down. A thought flashes through my mind of me at 7 or 8 years old. My mom had experienced a miscarriage and was not coping very well. I remember she was crying and came and laid down on the sofa in the living room. She told me something along the lines that she was going to sleep and not waking up. Everything was in 'This letter!' She set the letter down, told me I could read it if I wanted to, rolled over and went to sleep. Fortunately for her, I was advanced in reading and could read it well enough to understand what it said. She had left a suicide note for my father explaining how unhappy she was with everything. Most of it I didn't understand, but I understood enough to know that she had taken pills. That she didn't think she needed to be here with us anymore. She was going to die and get away from the things that were hurting her. I immediately ran upstairs to the phone in their bedroom and dialed '411'. I don't know if '911' existed yet; this would have been about 1975 or 1976 and it was limited in different parts of the United States. I did know how to use Information: my parents often let me get the numbers of restaurants or movie theatres when we needed them. I tell the 411 operator I need the phone number for Ann and Abraham Makler. She replies that the number is unlisted. I repeat myself because I don't understand what she means. She then explains that Ann and Abraham don't want to give their number out. I tell her that's 'Silly!' I am sure if she will just tell Ann it's me, Stacey, she would want me to have the number. The operator is telling me it doesn't work that way. I remember starting to feel very flush in the face and starting to cry. I began giving the operator details to prove I was the granddaughter. Saying things like 'If you tell my grandma it's Stacey with the long red hair, I know she would, won't you give me the number!!!' I am rattling off details, all of a sudden I hear my grandma's voice on the other end of the phone! I guess the operator had called her, explained the situation and put my call through. I tell my grandma what's happening. My grandma and my dad show up and they take care of my mom. I remember them making her walk around and giving her sips of soda to drink. Them telling her to 'Do it for your daughter!' Her telling them, 'Let me sleep, in a year Stacey won't remember me!' My parents divorced about a year later and I lived with my dad. Suicide in my dad's world was never brought up; it wasn't talked about in front of me, and it certainly wasn't anything he considered as an answer. I also never did forget that day and how it made me feel.

My mom went on to remarry and have my younger brother. I remember visiting them on a summer vacation when I was 17 years old and my brother was 5 years old. My mom and step-dad had a big fight over something trivial. I thought it would be over in a little while, but that was not the case. My step-dad had locked himself in the bathroom and was threatening to kill himself! My mom was banging on the bathroom door, begging him to come out! My step-dad is screaming NO, he is going to cut his wrists! Eventually my little brother is at the door crying, begging his daddy to please come out! After about an hour of all of us begging, my step-dad comes out and tells us all how wrong we were to argue with him in the first place. These episodes continued throughout most of my brother's younger childhood. His father threatening to jump out of moving cars. My mom having to call the paramedics to get his father out of a locked bathroom.

Sadly on top of that, suicide seemed to run in the men in my step-dad's family. On several occasions when my brother was young they would let him overhear conversations about suicides of uncles that he didn't know and had never met. Going over the gory details, with my young brother seven or eight feet away watching cartoons. I would offer to take my brother out of the room, but he didn't want to go, and they didn't force him. They would tell me that he was watching cartoons, and not to worry. What he was doing was straining to hear snippets of information. 'He just couldn't take it anymore!', 'Well it wasn't his first try!', 'You couldn't even recognize the body' and 'Sad, never thought he would really end up doing it.' My brother's eyes would get wide with interest and fear. As an adult these incidents kept happening. The years leading up to my brother's death, his uncle committed suicide with a shotgun in his bedroom, while his wife was in the living room. He also had a cousin (related to that uncle, his eldest son) who ran himself into a freeway divider.

Did my brother seeing and hearing about suicide so many times in life learn that it was a very available option or way out? Were our experiences with watching the people we love try to hurt themselves so very different that we learned two very different lessons? Did I misunderstand or did he misunderstand? For once in my life I am glad this is a lesson I do not and did not understand.

From sisterhood to suicide:
The story of a suicide loss

Cath Walsh

I had a little sister. For as long as I can remember, I identified with Shirley Hughes' *My Naughty Little Sister* books. What I am writing here is as much as I can remember of what I experienced over 25 years. Some of my memories may be hazy, and may not be what other people knew or remembered. I don't claim that I was the perfect individual – we are how we are as situations occur in our lives – but I don't intend anything I write to be an opportunity to tarnish her memory; it is just as it was. I suppose it is my own journey – from sisterhood to suicide.

Even from a young age, she was incredibly dominant, demanding and attention seeking. I was by no means perfect, but already being a quieter individual, I went the other way, demanding very little, not asking for things because I felt like I had to be good to balance out the demands. Things became more noticeably wrong once she began secondary school, turned vegetarian and then began ruling and controlling via food and self-harming, though she was never suicidal.

She was very sporty and athletic and had a short hairstyle. Aged about 11, she was stopped going into the toilet by a prefect, who informed her she was going into the Ladies and gave her a hard time, before realising she was a girl. After that, she grew her hair long, wore the shortest skirts, the highest heels and so much lipstick, almost like she was painting on a smile. She always looked up to older people and desperately tried to fit others' perceptions of what was cool. I was recently discussing this with my parents, and for a long time allowed myself to feel bad because I wasn't the big sister she wanted, that her issues were my fault, and her need to feel loved was because she didn't feel loved by me – but it wasn't even a big sister or a mother figure that she wanted to replace; she just wanted to feel loved and protected, and looked after to such a degree that no single relationship or friendship could have been enough. One of the last conversations I remember was that she said she just wanted to go home and be looked after, and I've finally come to realise that was what she was always looking for – being sheltered from the realities of the world, because she couldn't cope with what was out there.

I spent a good proportion of our early teenage years listening to her scream and shout while I was in another room, shut out. I knew something was going on, not least because of the blood-stained tissues, the long sleeves in summer and the explosions at meals, if she ate with us. By 14 she had given up athletics due to problems with her feet and legs, but it was almost like she didn't believe she was any good at it. That seemed to be the case a lot – she started something but if things started to go wrong, she needed someone to carry on for her, to finish the job.

Despite the constant battles and feelings of being a failure, she still did incredibly well at 16, and again at 18 – her results being far better than mine. She was in Mauritius on results day, and when she came back to get ready for university, she suddenly went into melt-down. It was almost like she was so convinced she would fail, she hadn't been prepared for the fact she was going to pass and go to university – York St John to study Occupational Therapy. After some intense therapy, she managed to get herself ready to go with our parents' support. When she was ill, she would blame them for making her do it – but she was so desperate to do it at the time, that they just wanted to give her every opportunity they could. Either way they could not win – if they hadn't got her there, I'm sure she would have blamed them for that.

She was mid-way through the course, achieving amazing grades, but just didn't seem to be able to cope. She arrived at home in February for a holiday after finishing a mental health placement – and never went back, other than to collect her belongings. I had been to visit just a few weeks before and, while we had a good time, she seemed quite fragile and snappy with her flatmates, spending hours listening to depressing music or sleeping. At the time she complained that people were not very supportive but I think they were just at the end of their tether from trying to support her and it never being enough.

After a few months recovering, she started several jobs and was amazingly well thought of and successful – but each time, something went wrong and she couldn't cope. For someone who craved being looked after, she often did extremely brave things, including working as a nanny in the French Alps. It wasn't what she expected and she left because she couldn't manage the expectations and extreme living conditions. After that, she really went downhill. I was in my final year of university and ended up deferring my final teaching placement because the combination of the school I was in, and what was going on with her, just stopped me from being able to do it all. It got to the point where she wouldn't go out and would sleep all day or sit in the corner, crying on the cat, if someone so much as looked at her for too long, or screamed if you dared to suggest you weren't going to do what she desired.

She was diagnosed with an anxiety disorder but seemed to experience physical pain, particularly if going out, even to the doctors. I don't know what drugs she took but, despite the support from the GP and a therapist, nothing was working. She opted to go into hospital for six months, then to sheltered living where she was responsible for her shopping, food and washing. Then she went into a shared supported house and, finally, her own flat with community support.

In the beginning, she functioned well, and had only short hospital stays. She volunteered at a therapy garden, and with 'Headway', who were so impressed with her, they offered her a management role. But she found she couldn't cope with the responsibility and it came crashing down. She realised she couldn't manage a full-time job. She had also started therapeutic artwork and glass painting with our cousin, Cathy. She developed amazing skills and people were commissioning and buying her work, and she won awards from the art community. But even that became stressful when she had to decide between making a living or doing it for therapeutic earnings. She seemed to feel she couldn't cope with life like others could, struggling to manage work, balanced relationships and the things that she was seeing her friends do easily. She'd had a great outlet through the mental health team and got involved – only for the funding to be withdrawn. Most of the groups ran for a few weeks or ended completely, and all that she was really left with was the day centre – which essentially gave her a view of a future which was less than appealing. I seem to recall that she had always been positive, even when she was ill. It was like she still felt there was hope for the future and that, when she felt better, she would have loads to offer. But then it started to change and she became very brittle and impatient with anyone who had a problem.

Things really changed when she had her wisdom teeth out. She had waited all day, and was in pre-op, when they cancelled the surgery due to the surgeon having had an accident. That was entirely out of anyone's control – but with more careful management, she could have had the procedure at 8 a.m. to reduce her anxiety levels. So she waited a further two months and went through the whole anxiety again. After the general anaesthetic, she really changed and the personality disorder became very obvious. Much of the behaviour we saw as a really young child – tantrums, threatening things to get her own way – started happening again. She showed a child-like dependency and fear of abandonment – she became physically abusive when she couldn't get her own way, rang up to 20 or 30 times a day, leaving inappropriate voice messages. We eventually unplugged our phones and got new mobile SIM cards so we could stay in contact. I had just finished teaching one lunchtime when she sent me a text saying Mum had suffered a stroke. I went into panic mode. By a stroke of luck, Dad had just plugged the phone in so Mum could ring him from work. It didn't make sense as Mum was apparently in a different hospital to the one she was working near, but there was the worry that the hospital might have been trying to get hold of us. Fortunately, Mum rang when she went on her break, but it really was the final straw for me. I knew my sister was ill but that was just a step too far. If we hadn't been able to get hold of Mum, I would not have been in any fit state to go back into the classroom. I began to feel that her actions were impacting on my life, despite the distance.

There was another big change after her wisdom teeth came out. She had always looked immaculate. I think it was perhaps the mask on what was really lying beneath. But then she started looking different, really old and worn. She stopped caring for the lovely flat she had. There was mouldy food and plates left for weeks, cigarette butts in piles everywhere. She wanted to get rats and get evicted she could 'go home' and be looked after – she just wanted to be a baby again. Mum and Dad had supported her for so long; there was no way she could go home. Being able to unplug the phone was about the only respite they had, and even then they were still wondering what would happen when they plugged it in. Perhaps some people will think they should have taken her in, but they won't be people who have ever experienced the situations we did. Ultimately she was an adult; she had support from the community team, and a lot of support from family and friends. After 25 years of her, I was really worried Mum and Dad would die from the stress they were under. I had already seen it make Mum ill over the years, the constant calls from school that she would get while she was at work, the screaming and tantrums at home, and the constant support with school and her school work. There is only so much support any parent or relative can give, and we were all at breaking point. I was lucky in some ways that I was living a long way off, but that also made it hard because I couldn't support them, I couldn't support her, and when I did see or talk to my parents they were too drained for us to really enjoy ourselves or have a proper conversation. I had been living with that for 25 years too.

Then she completely changed from the previous diagnosis she had been given, when she started making suicide attempts. Even though she had self-harmed, she had never been suicidal. The first attempt was in order to get attention from her CPN (community psychiatric nurse) who, of course, responded appropriately. She then made at least two more attempts in a week, disappearing from the hospital to buy cigarettes and not returning. She felt so bad about the reaction given to her in A&E, she just spiralled into self-destruct as she swayed from wanting people to look after her and guilt about having upset people. The worse she felt, the worse she behaved and so the less attention she got – and around it went. I remember being completely stunned she had done it. I wasn't told until the third attempt in the same week. It wasn't intentionally hidden from me but due to the roller-coaster Mum and Dad were on they never had time to call me in between. I was absolutely furious. It felt like more attention-seeking behaviour coming after the rest of what was going on. In addition, it was just before our first wedding anniversary and, perhaps selfishly, I was scared she was going to succeed on our day and ruin that for the rest of our lives, as she subsequently did with Valentine's Day. Our cousin was just about to have an operation for a brain tumour she had recently been diagnosed with and in the face of that battle for life, it just seemed like such an insult, not least because they had been close and she really supported Steph when she went into hospital the first time.

The Christmas before she died, we were with my in-laws, as we'd had the last two years with my folks. It was horrid – I wasn't sure what could have been worse – that my parents had to deal with her on their own – or being there and having to deal with it too.

Just after Christmas, Mum and Dad came up to stay with us. There was a battle even before they arrived because she wanted to come with them, even though she was invited for New Year. Mum and I were making the most of the sales, and were just in the second shop, when I got a text from my husband saying she was ringing the house but they were ignoring it. Then both our phones kept ringing so eventually I answered. She asked me where the hell we were and when I told her, she screamed at me to put Mum on. I told her Mum was in the changing rooms so would ring her back, and hung up, but she kept ringing. Mum finally told her very calmly that she would call her when we got back from shopping and that if she had a problem she needed to call the crisis team, but it absolutely floored her and we didn't even stay for lunch. I was livid because I had vouchers I wanted to spend and we had been having a proper good girly time. With living 150 miles apart, I never got to spend much time with Mum and Dad – she had ruined her own Christmas with them and was now ruining my time, as usual. I was really, really furious but I also saw just what it was doing to them. She didn't come for New Year and that was when we started getting bombarded so we unplugged the phones and got new SIM cards to enable contact without hearing from her. It sounds really mean now but it was impossible and there was constant abuse. I ended up off work with stress at the end of January and she would ring all day if I didn't unplug the phone.

The weekend before she died we were at a wedding, and I got a text from her telling me she had attacked Mum. On the Monday, she turned up at my parents, putting coke, crisps, shampoo, and who knows what else through the letterbox, singing, crying, shouting and hammering the door. My Dad was away and I got a call from Mum saying she had gone to a friend's house. I was absolutely terrified that Mum was going to go back to talk to her and get seriously hurt. Fortunately when she went back, Steph had gone to the shop so Mum was able to get into the house before she returned. She ended up being arrested for causing a public nuisance. I got calls from her begging me to talk to her and look after her, which then turned into abusive texts when I told her what I thought of her behaviour. In the end, my husband just deleted any of the texts she had sent but did say they were just a barrage of insults and attacks on me. It was all pretty normal for her by then.

She died on 15th February 2007 – but we didn't find out until the following day. It was on the front of the *Surrey Advertiser* that someone had jumped at the car park – it was purely good luck that my parents didn't get the paper that day as they would have known.

I always wonder what happened to the person that found the body. They didn't realise at the time and just thought she had passed out – but they would have read about it. And I wonder about the police that had to watch the CCTV and then tell my parents. After, they rang us, and told Dave; it was the longest journey of my life.

It has had an enormous impact on all our lives. In some ways, it was a release of pain for not only her. She was at a point where she was in physical pain from the effort of carrying on. With a physical illness, eventually the body gives up when the pain gets too great, but with a mental illness the body just carries on. Even though it left a gaping hole, we were finally all at peace from the constant worry and wonder of 'what next?'

I remember when we were telling the families that we were expecting – it felt wrong not telling her – and when the children arrived. It breaks my heart to think they will never have my sister, their aunt, at their celebrations. For all her faults when she was ill, she would have been totally fantastic as she loved babies. Except then my brain gives me dreams each time I miss her that are almost the future if she had not died – and I realise how awful it would probably have been. Mum and Dad are up here whenever they can be and have been, as any grandparent would, so joyful of their grandchildren. They would have missed out on that purely from the stress and exhaustion of dealing with what was going on. And I would never have trusted her because she would have been so jealous she would have been likely to hurt the baby because she didn't know any better in that state – like with her hurting my parents.

I try to think that from her death I gained some gifts. Because of the reactions my brain and body had, and from the experience of seeing what she went through, I became determined not to waste a second of my life. I found I needed to develop ways of looking after myself, including holistic therapies, yoga and reusing my skills to find a life that centres round me and the family as a whole. I might never have discovered so many of my talents, and met so many of the most amazing people, if I hadn't experienced such trauma.

For several years I went to local SOBS (Sharers of Bereavement by Suicide) group meetings. Sadly the group ended when people moved on, but I met some amazing people through that group and at least one great friend. Now I have such an extreme experience of loss, I hope it makes it more possible for me to support others in their hour of need – basing it on the ways that helped me, and having learned from what was less helpful.

I discovered that no matter what, the wedding vows we made were truly tested 'for worse', and now the 'for better' is out there for us to continue discovering and enjoying. The relationship I have with my oldest and best friend became even more vital and close than I could have expected it to. It has showed me real friends and highlighted the true importance of having the right people around me who are unconditionally supportive, as I try to be for them. I have also been able to regain the missing hours with my parents. And perhaps the fact I had to wait for these times makes them even better, as I get to share them with my children too.

In no possible way would I ever have wished that she was dead – what I always wished for was that she could be like other people's sisters, and happy. Since that was not her life experience, it has made me all the more determined that I make it mine.

Learning/discussion points:

- The way in which those who survive a suicide attempt are treated in Accident & Emergency units of hospitals needs greater attention, compassion and understanding. Greater respect should be shown to them and less personal judgement. Staff must understand that someone who attempts suicide is potentially or actually just as ill as any cancer or accident victim.

- More support should be given to families, post-suicide, including the provision of more support groups or at least people being signposted to the right places. The incidence of the suicide bereaved going on to commit suicide signals the need for greater suicide 'aftermath' support in the early days.

Untitled **7**

Catherine Carley

Looking in the mirror every morning I am reminded of my mum. The fact that I resemble her still catches me out, and that face looking back invites the sudden wave of grief that is a defining part of my daily life. My throat tightens, my mouth strains and I swallow back a whimper. I sniff and toss back my head and my eyes start to water.

Water, water everywhere. It's almost six years since my mum drowned. I have to make the distinction about the nature of her death because I believe there is meaning in how and why she died the way she did. The coroner recorded an open verdict so officially she didn't commit suicide but all that means really is they can't say one way or another what her intentions were. All they (and the police) could say with any degree of certainty is that there was no foul play involved. She was on her own. So an open verdict was the only verdict the coroner could reach. Despite the years of mental illness (clinical depression, schizophrenia and OCD), the spells in hospital and the previous suicide attempts (two overdoses using her prescription drugs and another encounter with water while attending an acute day centre she disappeared and was found laid down in a stream) her actual death was not recorded as suicide. I feel resigned to not knowing. It wasn't an accident though, it wasn't misadventure, it wasn't anything sinister – so there are certain things I can rule out.

Never truly knowing what happened is just something I have to accept. I know she caught the bus to Lodge Moor at about 10.30 a.m. on Saturday and I presume she walked from the terminus to Redmires. It was a week before Christmas and it was dark by 4 p.m. She was found by a passer-by around 9 a.m. on Sunday morning floating face down in the reservoir near the jetty. The coroner ascertained she had been in the water no longer than six hours so I have to accept that she did not enter the water until around 3 a.m. on Sunday morning. I have to accept that I'll never know what she was thinking and doing from getting off the bus at Lodge Moor terminus to taking her last breath in the freezing dark water high up above the city while I, equally high up but on the opposite side of town, lay wrapped in a duvet on the sofa at my parents' house unable to sleep, helplessly hoping she was warm and safe somewhere.

They never found her bag. They never found her shoes. She was fully clothed in the water when she was found. The funeral director offered to dispose of her clothes by burning. You just nod in agreement to offers like that, assuming they know what's best.

On the first anniversary of her drowning I went to the reservoir to leave flowers and found it had been drained. My first instinct was to climb over the wall and run out onto the mud to look for her shoes and bag. Then reality hit. It was vast; it was unsafe; anything could be buried under the silty brown mud. What would looking have achieved? I knew deep down there was no explanation, there would be no clue to reveal a reason hidden in her bag. She would remain a secret and soon the water would come back and plenty of other secrets would stay hidden beneath its calm dark surface.

The whole day and night she was missing all I could think was that I hoped she was warm and safe. The fact she lost her shoes somewhere between leaving home at 10.30 on Saturday morning and being found in the reservoir at 9 on Sunday morning seems trivial but to me it's a reminder of her strength. A couple of years previously she spent the night standing barefoot in the garage on a freezing concrete floor convinced that she was the only thing stopping the house from exploding. Her terrified face imploring me to get back in the kitchen and shut the door as the garage was pressurised and she needed all her powers of concentration to control the pressure. At that moment my concern for her cold feet did not register with her; neither did my concern for her mental health as she was completely gone. That night was the closest we came to getting her sectioned. I don't know how he did it but my younger brother patiently coaxed her back inside where, seated on a dining room chair, I put her socks back on as two community psychiatric nurses looked on.

Me and Dad sat on the sofa side by side while three police officers filled up the front room. My aunt and uncle came running up the road when they saw the police cars pull up in the quiet cul-de-sac. We all knew instinctively what the news was. Still, they have to tell you; it has to be said out loud for you to hear, for your brain to register, for your heart to crack and for your throat to let out that noise. My brother and sister weren't there. It would be my job to tell them. It would be my job to tell my husband and our two sons too.

I remembered being with my sister in my house on Boxing Day morning seven years earlier when she received the news that her boyfriend back in France had died. He'd fallen or jumped from their fourth floor balcony to the street below. He had been severely depressed. It was a night of fierce storms in France with trees falling and roof tiles flying. There was no suicide note. The coroner recorded an open verdict. So for the second time in her life my sister absorbed the shock and the blow of another suicide of a loved one. She had just become a mother for the first time six weeks earlier, and a week before our mum died her partner's father also died. Just recounting this again makes me marvel at our capacity to endure and to keep going knowing that there's light after the dark and that there are always possibilities, even if included in those possibilities is to take your own life.

The days following her death were surreal. I had to buy the children suits for the funeral, fielding work phone calls in Debenhams' changing rooms. I'm self-employed so there's no 'Sorry, I've got to take time off for a while.' I went into Jones and bought some new shoes and blurted out they were for my mum's funeral. The shop assistant burst into tears. A job I was doing, publicity for a beautiful film installation by Bill Viola, featured a person sinking under water then surfacing in a perpetual loop. My head was filled with constant images running through the sequence of events of the weekend.

Thank god we had the Christmas holiday but fuck Christmas, we had the mortuary to visit, we had a funeral to organise, we had newspaper notices to write and police to check in with. In a complete daze I picked my sister and her partner up from the airport and gazed at my new nephew's content little face wondering how on earth all this was going on.

If there was one thing I knew I had to do, it was to speak at the funeral. I wrote out of grief, anger and a wall of insurmountable sadness. There was something driving me to speak up now, to tell whoever cared to listen that my mum counted and that there was no shame in what happened. I didn't want someone else to speak on my behalf. I'd been to funerals when whoever was conducting the service put together some appropriate words after a brief chat with the bereaved relatives, but I didn't think anyone would be able to translate what was going through my head. This was so important, so deeply personal. My brother and sister supported my decision and contributed their own memories for me to include. Here is the speech exactly as I wrote it.

When I was little, I hated carrots. They were my least favourite vegetable but they kept turning up on my plate week in, week out without fail. There was no escaping them. I could try and leave them to the end, but by the time I'd got through everything else they'd be cold. And there's only one thing worse than hot carrots – cold carrots. They weren't going away. I wasn't going to be let off the hook.

Mashed potatoes on the other hand I could eat until they came out of my ears. Funny, the same people who gave me the awful carrots also fed me the heavenly mashed potatoes. Those same people taught me that if I mashed the few awful carrots into the mountain of potatoes it would make the horror of the carrots easier to swallow.

It's a simple lesson and one of the first I learned (albeit with much stroppiness) but it's what I'm going to fall back on to get me through today and the coming days.

I might look like Linda's girl but looking back it was always me and Dad walking ahead with Mum and Claire, and then James dawdling behind. It wasn't easy being patient for the slowcoaches back then and it hasn't been easy finding the strength and patience to cope with Mum's decline into depression, especially early on when her health became a cause for concern and nothing was making sense.

After working so hard for so long all Dad wanted was to spend his retirement with Mum together, and what should have been a golden time of sitting back and enjoying life, watching their children and grandchildren grow up, not worrying what was over the horizon, suddenly became a very different landscape.

The depression that descended on her was an illness as real as any cancer, heart attack or stroke, as painful as a body of broken bones. For Mum it was fatal. It tormented her for years and made her life unbearable. It took her away from us on more occasions than I want to remember. We were there for her all the time, she just couldn't let anyone in. I believe in my heart that she knew how much we all loved her and I think she felt guilty for all the chaos and pain that her illness caused the people around her. Never mind the anguish, confusion and fear she was going through herself. All we wanted was for you to get better. All I wanted was my mum back.

There were times it looked brighter. There were times over the past few years when you came back. When you didn't look scared, when you seemed able to relax, when you'd approach life with a rare enthusiasm. Those times were precious and Dad would make the most of them usually with a holiday somewhere warm and sunny with good friends for company. You'd swim in the sea, enjoy good food, beautiful scenery and just live for the day. Because really, Mum, you had everything you needed to make you happy. Nobody could explain why it kept slipping from your grasp; it just did.

The times she spent in hospital were always a last resort and were very hard to bear. But the staff took good care of her and helped her gradually to come back home to Dad and some kind of normality. She was helped particularly by going to the Moncrieffe Centre where she found space and spent time painting and learnt chi gong, which she insisted we all try.

My mum died because she was ill. I don't know why she became ill but the depression she suffered was what killed her.

I don't know why it was that particular Saturday that she chose to take herself up to Redmires. I don't know what she thought to herself as she stood at the water's edge. I don't know what went through her mind as she took her last breath and gave herself up to the icy water. I don't know much at all.

I can't find the right words and I'm scared I'll always be looking for them because I don't think there is an answer. There's simply no explanation, no logic, no rhyme or reason to your death. All I know is it is over now and you found peace. All I know is we have to carry on without you.

This is what I know. What I remember.

Walking to school holding your hand. Summer lunchtimes when me and Claire would meet you in the park for a picnic. Watching you sleep on a Saturday afternoon while Dad was at football, rollers in your hair because you were going out later.

Singing, always singing. 'I wanna be your Kookachoo' by Alvin Stardust with your rubber gloves on, chasing me into bed.

Dancing with everyone at our wedding. Being at the birth of my second son, Patrick. Your first comment, 'He looks like Charles Bronson!' The boys singing a song they'd made up for you, a calypso called 'There's an energetic Grandma running round the beach eating sausages'.

Claire remembers the first Mother's Day present she made for you, peppermint fondants in an egg box lined with purple tissue paper. You never forgot them and no subsequent present could beat them. For Claire you were always young at heart. Your ability to laugh and joke with our friends made us proud to introduce this beautiful lady as our mum.

For James the most important thing was that you insisted our happiness was paramount. That was all that mattered to you, that your children were happy whatever they did, wherever they found themselves in life. You taught all of us not to judge and you led by example. You were genuine and true, kind and generous.

Dad had a nickname for you. It was Mabel. I thought it was just a silly name because he's like that, but it wasn't at all. One day you showed me a cotton handkerchief with a letter M embroidered on it. Dad had found it on your honeymoon and presented it to you as a gift. The 'M' you both decided stood for 'Mabel'. You were silly, affectionate, romantic and in love. The fact you kept that hanky for nearly 45 years is a tiny detail of your life that speaks volumes. All I can say about my dad is that no one comes close to him, and no one loved you like he loved you.

Mum, all the clever things you said, all the good advice you gave, all the support and understanding you offered will be missed by so many people. I really don't think you realised how much you counted and how beautiful you were. Goodbye my beautiful Mum.

Nearly 300 people attended City Road crematorium to pay their respects to her and to show support for our family. Among family, friends, work colleagues and neighbours was a long-time friend of mine, Kathryn. Kathryn and I go back a long way and with any luck will go on for a good few more years. She is a diamond, unique, multifaceted, and has strength formed by compression with the earth. She lights up a room when she enters it. She came to my mum's funeral in spite of the fact she could barely walk, regardless of the fact that there would quite possibly be people there who weren't comfortable with her presence, and despite the fact that, not long before, she narrowly avoided being in the coffin at the centre of everyone's attention due to reasons not dissimilar to my mum's reason for being there.

If there has been one person with whom I have shared this experience most, it is Kathryn. She did her very best to kill herself and failed, leaving her with a body that bit by bit amazing surgeons put back together and she, knowing that this was how it was going to be from then on, pushed and heaved and through sheer willpower got her body and her mind (let's not forget that) back into working order. Different from before, but working nonetheless.

Water water everywhere. Kathryn's collision with the earth resulted in pushing her toward water, for the only real exercise she is able to do is in the swimming pool. I started accompanying her to the pool every Saturday by way of encouragement and as a good excuse to catch up each weekend. It became a bit of a habit. We both loved swimming but only now after over 25 years of friendship have we found this activity that we do together which helps keep both of us sane. I enjoy the meditative aspect of counting laps and strokes and the way it allows me to empty my head of daily stresses. I must admit that in a macabre way it makes me think about drowning. If I accidentally swallow a mouthful of water I instinctively cough it back out and pull up for a breath. Then I wonder what it would take to cut out the impulse to survive, or how it would feel to be overcome with the sheer exhaustion of trying to stay above water, of keeping going, of breathing, of living. Then I carry on swimming.

Look at me, not drowning but waving.

8

Gone but not forgotten

Georgina Smith

It's the anniversary of his death. My boyfriend, John, committed suicide by jumping off a multistorey car park, and the events of that day are as clear in my mind as if it had happened yesterday – the shock, numbness, devastation, fear of the future – how would I cope without him?

People have started calling it 'The Strawberry Jam Case' which I find quite hurtful. However, I can't do much about it and I suppose it describes what people found when they arrived at the scene. I'm so glad I didn't see that.

He was in a psychiatric hospital suffering from depression and we had agreed that I would visit for just ten minutes each evening. When people are in a psychiatric hospital they often find it hard to cope with visitors and don't feel like making conversation. This was why we decided to limit my visits to just ten minutes. It was very important to us, as boyfriend and girlfriend, to see each other every day.

One evening, as I arrived and was signing in, a nurse came to me saying that John's nurse wanted to see me and would I please wait in the quiet room.

'What's all this about?' I wondered as I sat there. 'Was he not well enough to see me?' Many thoughts went through my head.

I knew John's nurse, and when he came into the room he had a devastated expression on his face. Something was obviously seriously wrong. He asked if I had listened to the radio or seen the local paper. I hadn't.

'I'm sorry,' he said. 'I've got some very bad news for you. John died earlier today when he jumped off a multistorey car park in town.'

I said nothing. It was such a shock and I was numb. I just sat there. In the end the nurse called my friend who took me to her house to care for me, but I couldn't talk about what had happened. I stayed there until the funeral and then gradually moved back home.

At the funeral I just sat there silently with tears streaming down my face. I recognised several people at the funeral, but I couldn't speak to them as I was overcome by my own grief.

His body was completely destroyed so I couldn't see it. It would have given me a sense of closure.

All that is left is a small plaque on a wall of remembrance at the crematorium with his name on. At first I couldn't go to see it, it was all too much. However, John's nurse said he would come with me that first time and I was very grateful to him, especially as he was doing it in his own time.

Now I go myself and find it helpful to sit there remembering John. Sometimes I cry as I remember the good times we had together that we will never have again. I know he's not there, but it's one place I can go which means something to me.

It still affects me now. It dominates my dreams and I find it hard to talk about. I've just started telling close friends about bits of it. Writing this has been quite painful, but also therapeutic. All this has thrown up questions for me, such as:

I was very close to John and I'm fearful of what might happen if I form another close relationship. Will I ever be able to form a lasting relationship again? Perhaps I'm not ready to move on yet as my grief is still so raw.

Who knows, time will tell.

Some emerging learning/discussion points:

- It is positive that John's nurse broke the news to me as he was the person who knew us best.

- Should the nurse in charge have let John go out? On the other hand, to what extent was it possible to detect that he was suicidal?

9

Untitled

Alex

Some time in December 2010

*It's coming up to a year since my mum tried to kill herself.
No one has really talked about it since it happened, and
apart from my diary I've never told anyone the full details
of what happened. So I'm getting flashbacks most days and
when they start it's impossible to stop until I've lived
through the whole episode again. It's like I need to get it
out of me but I can't and every time I try and write about it
nothing comes and I find it impossible to talk about it except
in indirect fragments of 'when that happened'. And I feel
so guilty like it's crawling into my throat and pushing
against the inside of my head until I just have to forget
about it for as long as possible. I'm the parent and I have
to stop them from fighting and killing themselves and I bury
my head in sand until everything hits me again and the
flashbacks start. There was no question of giving in. My
sister refused to come home, my little brother couldn't
handle going over, and she's completely estranged from
her family.*

*And so I'm here. And I can't even express how I felt
when I saw her and thought she was dead. Or what I
imagined I'd find on the drive over. Or when I found all
the suicide notes with our names on and had to hide them.
That's kind of how I feel.*

I said ambulance, please. An ambulance. Repeat the address
please. Of course, yes. Thank you. Are her airways blocked?
Can you check? Yes I'm checking; no they're not blocked.
She started to wake up and started to groan.

Sun 3rd Jan 2010

I can't shake the thought of her on that sofa and her crying and pleading to die in the ambulance. I can't hide it when I look in her eyes. I have to look away. I don't want her to see it but it concerns me that she has no idea of the magnitude of what she's done. I feel like there's no one I can trust.

The drive across town was erratic; there was no music playing so the only sounds came from my head and from the car. It takes about 25 minutes at least to get from one parent's house to the other, but it may as well have been hours. All the way I had no idea what I'd be met with when I walked through the door. It was like watching a nightmare with different endings. The likelihood was that she'd be drunk and it was all just a misinterpretation of a cryptic text. I'd scream at her for terrifying me and we'd fall out for a while but it would be all right. Maybe it was the panic before I left, but I don't know if I'd have driven over by myself or if I'd have rung for an ambulance beforehand if I'd seriously considered the idea that she might have tried to kill herself. What if those 25 minutes had made the difference? There'd been no hesitation from when there was no answer from her phone. I'd go as fast as I could and wouldn't speak to anyone until I'd seen it.

Sat 2nd Jan 2010

She managed to say sorry and thank you but hasn't talked about the overdose except to say that she won't do it again. She fitted about six times today (as far as I know) which was a fucking awful thing to watch.

We went walking over the top in the dark with the dog, through the snow. I said I should probably call my mum and wish her a happy new year because I hadn't spoken to her since Christmas Eve. The party carried on when we got back inside. It was New Year's Day and we were still rough around the edges from the night before. Someone was cooking and Guitar Hero had been abandoned, sound still on, in the living room. I was adding photos to Facebook from the night before and drinking my first beer of the evening. I had a message from my mum's boyfriend.

In the kitchen my friends were still making dinner, and in the living room Guitar Hero was still playing and in the other room my dad and brother were still watching a film. I told my friends I had to go out and that if my dad asked then I left something at a friend's house and needed it back. Someone asked me if I was all right and I said I didn't know.

Tues 5th Jan 2010

I saved her life and I'm there every day trying to help and she can't even sit next to me. I don't even want to get up in the morning, let alone be in that house. I resent it and I hate it but I'm doing it because I don't want her to die and I'm one of the only people she's got. It might feel better if I felt I was closer to anything.

My dad and brother were already at the hospital before the ambulance managed to get there. I hastily gave my mum's details to the receptionist in A&E, and I remember the waiting room being pretty empty except for a few people watching us, no questions asked. There was a long wait before any of us were allowed to see her. The nurses were having trouble getting her to respond to anything so they took my dad in first to see if he could get any consciousness out of her. The mixture of drugs and alcohol was taking effect and all she was doing was squirming around on her bed trying to get comfortable enough to sleep it off, and occasionally being still. I held her hand gently, without response back. She was unable to talk and didn't seem to have any idea of where she was. When she began to keep more still, I whispered to her to grab my hand if she could hear me and if she knew who I was. There was a small grab, just soft enough to feel but firm enough to seem intentional.

Sat 2nd Jan 2010

I just keep running through my head – her on New Year's Day getting drunk and crying and making that decision. I don't want to see or talk or spend time with anyone because it feels like I'm trying to escape the fact of what happened. Which is that my mum hated her life so much that she wanted it to end.

Two screams came out of my mouth when I walked into the living room. After I'd unlocked the door I went into the wrong room first, so I tried the kitchen and then through into the room where I found her. I thought she was dead. She was lying on the sofa with her left arm out, stretched over the side. Neither scream woke her up or even stirred her. There must have only been a few seconds between screaming and running over to her. There was a pulse. There was a pulse. There was a pulse. I felt embarrassed that I'd told the operator that my mum had taken an overdose before I managed to tell them what emergency services I needed. I said ambulance, please. An ambulance.

Fri 1ˢᵗ Jan 2010

Mum tried to kill herself today. Had a Facebook message about 9 p.m.
from her boyfriend saying she'd sent a really heavy text so I sped there
going out of my fucking mind. Went through the door shouting to find
her unconscious on the sofa. I screamed and checked her pulse. She
had one and was still breathing so I called an ambulance. There was
an empty bottle of pills, a bottle of alcohol and a half-drunk glass of
something along with suicide notes addressed to her boyfriend, my
dad, my sister, me, and my brother. The woman on the phone told me to
lay her out and keep her head back. She started to come round a bit by
the time the ambulance arrived. She protested a lot going in the
ambulance, basically crying and pleading them to leave her. Her friends
were outside waiting. Called everyone throughout. She told me she
loved us. That's the last I really spoke to her. Going back tomorrow. I
don't know what to feel or what to do with the notes.

I didn't know what to do with the notes. I'd spotted them while on the
phone to the emergency services. I knew that I shouldn't read them,
because it seemed like they weren't mine to read and I was terrified that
I would read something that I could never un-read. Before the ambulance
arrived I stashed them in my pocket in case they wanted to keep them,
and I didn't want that. So before I went in the ambulance I lifted the floor
off the boot of my car, undid the spare tyre and hid it far under where no
one would think to look. I convinced myself that if anyone else knew
they existed, they'd want to read them. Months later they told me that I
was right and they wouldn't have been able to stop themselves from
reading them, so maybe I did make the right decision. If they wanted to
read them I couldn't stop them, because their name was on their letter. I
just had to trust myself that they belonged to her as long as she was alive,
and not us.

The only part of the notes I remember was the names on them.
Sometime when I returned from hospital I took them out of the boot of
the car in secret, sealed them in an envelope with Sellotape and hid them
in the top part of my wardrobe underneath some spare bedding. Eventually
I decided that I would ask her if she wanted the notes back or if she
wanted me to destroy them, as soon as I could. She said that I should
destroy them, but I held off for a few days. Once she started some
counselling sessions at the local surgery, the time came where she asked
if she could have them back to help her remember what happened. One
afternoon when I left, I put the notes on the kitchen table, still sealed,
and she told me that they had helped after all.

Sat 2nd Jan 2010

She wasn't lucid enough for me to talk about the notes so I still have them stashed in my wardrobe. I feel bad that my brother and sister think that she would have killed herself without leaving us anything. They'll find out soon enough but now is not the right time.

The days in and out of hospital are the most blurry. She moved wards a lot, had lost all short-term memory, and part of her long-term memory. She wasn't conscious enough to have a proper conversation, let alone begin to understand why she was in hospital. She would begin to come round a little more, but was having regular fits in the recovering days; she started the cycle of forgetting and remembering all over again. Most of the time when I was there she was either unconscious or had forgotten too much to have a conversation with. I know very little of what had happened, medically. I think that her partner at the time had lied and told the hospital that they were married, since I was never given any information, let alone first, and he seemed to know what was happening.

Wed 27th Jan 2010

It's still tough. And the smell of the house freaks me out.

Love and support came from unexpected places in the weeks and months to come, as did pain and silence. The paramedics shrugged their shoulders when I asked them what I should do, but the receptionist at the local surgery showed some genuine empathy when I was lost and called to make an appointment for her. The doctors at her psychiatric assessment interrogated her so badly and gave her such conflicting diagnoses that she was too upset to return, but her GP took the time to call me back, to listen to her and make her feel like she was in safe hands. One of my departments on my course sent me a letter stating that 'there was no clear evidence of impairment in [my] results' and congratulated me 'on [my] achievement under extremely difficult circumstances', but my other department wrote off my exam and expressed their support for me throughout the rest of my time at university, considering what happened. My mum's then partner blamed me and my siblings for what happened, but one of my mum's friends shared her own story of her mother's suicide attempts with me.

Tues 2nd Feb 2010

Fred came over and we got drunk on beer and whisky. Talked about Stuff ... His godfather killed himself apparently. And I talked about

Mum. First time I've actually wanted to talk to anyone about it. It was good.

On October 12th, 2012 she's getting married again, to someone who took me aside one day to tell me how much he loves her and cares about her. I'm going to give her away.

Sat 9th Jan 2010

Today has been a lot better.

10

Suicidal wisdom

Jayne Stewart

My brother S was a gentle bear of a man, most of the time, and he loved his five children very much. He was happiest working outside in his organic garden; making beautiful and practical objects from reclaimed wood; cooking delicious food in his kitchen, or on a BBQ on the beach. He killed himself by overdosing in 1999. At the time I was very disturbed by his suicide and by other people's reactions to it, and the after-effects continue still.

We had a shared history of having been sexually abused by our father, J, but we had taken very different paths since recovering our memories of being abused. S was a psychiatric nurse and although it was hard for him to make the transition from being the 'professional' to being the 'patient', he chose to see a psychiatrist and took the drugs he was offered and ultimately used them to kill himself. I took an alternative route – initially because when I went to see my GP with depression after my son was born, there was no counselling service available and I was advised to see a psychotherapist privately. This was the start of a long and winding journey through many alternative and complementary ways of working with my traumatic childhood experiences.

S and I supported each other in many ways though it wasn't always easy. He was often very angry and physically and verbally attacked those he felt were responsible for his pain … and sometimes also those he loved. He attacked himself too – the one he found hardest to love and often blamed – putting himself down and cutting into his own flesh. The worst incident was one night when he ended up with his hands round his wife's neck trying to throttle her – he was in an altered state and only came out of it when their baby son woke up and started crying. He hated himself afterwards. The fact that he was hurting those he loved and couldn't stop himself was one of the reasons he gave for wanting to kill himself.

He didn't realise how much his death would also hurt us …

His death *did* also bring some relief for me and for others – not having to be with his extreme states of rage and withdrawal or deal with his increasing use of alcohol, and not going mad with worry each time he 'disappeared' for a few days was a relief. His death brought a lot of secrets out into the open which was also relieving for some of us, and distressing for others.

The long-term disturbance in the family has been huge. One of his daughters has a long-term diagnosis of anorexia and is struggling to reclaim her life and to be there for her own children; there has been a split in the family so some of us don't have any contact with each other anymore. This is particularly distressing for my mother, who has had no contact with S's two youngest children for several years now, because one of my sister's sons invited his grandfather, J, mine and S's father/ abuser, to his wedding. We were accused by S's wife of welcoming J back into the family, but actually what happened was that he was made painfully aware of how much his abuse has set him apart from the rest of the family. We all sat together and J was placed as far away from us as possible and most of us did not speak to him at all. He declined the next invitation to a family wedding.

The pain persists and the grief recurs and so does the disturbance – it is not only in the past: it is fully present each time there is a family gathering and discussions have to be had about who is or isn't invited, every time we go to visit some of my brother's children and don't see the others; and every time my niece shares her distress at being in hospital not able to look after her own children …

However, this pain and disturbance is not the whole story – I have also found ways to make meaning for myself out of my experience and to help others affected by suicide. This is an ongoing journey of reclaiming my sense of self and discovering my own medicine. It has been a physical, psychological and spiritual voyage; a dancing path back and forth between psychological emergency and spiritual emergence. A path made by walking, through remembering and forgetting, through forgiveness and rage, through loss and retrieval, letting go and holding on.

This reclamation began in 1997 following a 'Heartbeat' dance workshop exploring our emotions. During the workshop I had a powerful realisation that it was hard for me to move on with my life, because so much of my attention was on my past, so I decided, after many years of having no contact with my father, that I wanted to go and see him again and talk to him about how his behaviour had affected me. This was quite a challenge as he has always denied the abuse! With the support and encouragement of my dancing community, friends and family, I went ahead and succeeded in having a dialogue with him across our irreconcilable differences – a dialogue which has continued, infrequently, ever since and has been a significant part of my journey of recovery. I subsequently wrote about this experience for the Forgiveness Project and my story featured in a 3 Minute Wonder programme on the theme of forgiveness for Channel 4, which was shown in July 2006 on the first anniversary of the London Bombings. I wouldn't say I have forgiven J for having abused me and S; it is unforgivable, and some days I wake up and I still hate him, but the dialogues have been helpful and healing. Talking to my father has enabled me to do what I was not able to do as a child – to speak about how the abuse affected me; to make clear boundaries between us and to reclaim my power as an adult rather than feeling like a vulnerable child a lot of the time.

Understandably not everyone in my family likes me seeing my father – some of them see it as colluding with the enemy. It is important to say at this point that S and I reported the abuse to the social services soon after recovering our memories of it, and they and the police instigated measures to restrict J's contact with children, though there was not enough evidence, 30 years on, to proceed with a court case.

S found my visits impossible to understand – he was still furious with J and had been sending angry letters to him and other members of his small village community. However, a few weeks before he killed himself he rang J and asked to meet him. Perhaps not surprisingly, J refused as he was afraid that S's intention was to harm him, maybe even to kill him, though he has since wondered whether S might still be alive if he had agreed to meet him. We will never know. I continued to visit my father, once or twice a year, after S killed himself, which was viewed by some members of my family as a betrayal of S as well as collusion. From my perspective my visits are a way to keep bringing the ongoing effects of his abuse to J's attention and are a part of my spiritual practice.

A few days after S's funeral when I was feeling disturbed by various people's concern that I too might kill myself I went for a ride on the back of a friend's motorbike and asked him to take me somewhere where we could safely go fast enough for me to feel whether or not I wanted to live. The answer then was a clear Yes! And this yes to choosing to live my life creatively has continued throughout my ongoing exploration of the process of living and dying. Since then I have often asked myself why I am alive when S is dead. The answers have led me to engage in a conscious process of deciding what in my life wants to live more and what needs to die in order for this new life to flourish.

Movement has been my best medicine. The weekend S killed himself I was on a dance workshop which I had organised. The theme was the relationship between feminine and masculine energies. It began on a Friday night and my brother had already been missing for two days, since he had a row with his wife at the school gates after dropping his youngest son off for his first day at school. It still makes me cry to remember this bit: I started crying as soon as I began dancing and in the opening circle I said that my brother was missing and that I was afraid for him. When I got home there was a message on my answering machine to say S had been found and was being taken to hospital. I rang my sister-in-law. 'He's dead ...,' she said. I yelled, 'Don't lie to me! ...', refusing to believe what I already knew was true. For the rest of the evening I cried and yelled and howled at the moon and was held and held and held ... And the next day the women were dancing separately from the men and I danced and cried and was held again and again by the dancers and by the dance. And I am still dancing and I still cry sometimes and however I am feeling I am still held. And these days I am also teaching a creative, spiritual and therapeutic dance practice to others.

Before the funeral I went to see S's body – there were things I wanted to say to him. And it turned out he had things to 'say' to me too – such as to 'talk to that guy Arny Mindell; you are always going on about how to make sure this doesn't happen again.' I wasn't sure exactly what 'this' was, but synchronously I had just arranged to have my first session with a practitioner of Mindell's Process Oriented Psychology (Process Work, PW) – telling her that for the first time I was not starting therapy because I was in crisis, but because I was curious about PW, since I was given one of Mindell's books for my 40th birthday. The date of my first session turned out to be the day after I returned home from the funeral. How wrong I was about being in crisis! And again how held I felt. I wrote to Arny Mindell, telling him about what had happened and I have been studying PW both formally and informally ever since. It has saved my life and helped parts of me to die many times since that first session.

In 2009 I began a collaborative action research project exploring the process of suicide with a friend, H, who has also been personally affected by suicide and is both a Process Worker and an art therapist. We used movement and art-making and developed PW exercises to separate out and explore the relationship between the one who kills and the one who is killed, and to discover what the essential qualities were that needed more life and what part(s) needed to die in order for the whole person to live more fully. Initially we made a short video poem about S's suicide which we presented at the international PW conference in 2010. The feedback we received was very positive and we decided to continue the research. We have now made two more videos, one exploring our own suicidal processes and the other exploring suicides that have disturbed us. Both of these are based on exercises we have developed and we now use these exercises in Suicidal Wisdom (SW) workshops for people who have been affected by suicide and also for professionals who work with people affected by suicide.

My own suicidal feelings and fantasies are rare these days through having worked on them in this way. My most common fantasy involved me walking into a reservoir near where I live, with a large rock tied around my ankle and a knife in my hand to cut the rope if I change my mind! Whenever I ran the fantasy I always changed my mind and cut the rope, and when I did the SW exercise I discovered that the part of me that needs to die is the part that is dragged down into the depths by the weight of my trauma history and other people's reactions to it. This seems obvious, but it wasn't until I actually did the exercise and explored the scene in movement rather than as a visual fantasy that I really 'got it' in my body and was able to 'cut the rope' more consciously and then explore the new life which emerged. I found two new parts: one that is very skilled at exploring traumatic depths with wisdom and compassion, and a light, playful part who loves splashing about in the shallows and leaping and diving like a dolphin. These two have become my allies and allow me to engage deeply with the difficult and painful subject of suicide, and use my experiences to support others to explore their own disturbing experiences and discover the wisdom hidden in them.

S overdosed on a cocktail of drugs he had been prescribed over the years, mixed with alcohol, which he took on a remote beach. So even though he was still alive when he was found, it was too difficult to get him to an ambulance and he had to be taken by boat. He was dead before he got to hospital and at the inquest it was clear that because of the particular drugs he had taken, even if he had been found sooner, he would have been unlikely to survive. When I explored S's suicide the part that I found that needed to die was one who adapted to other people's views about how he should be and how he should behave. The part that needed to live more was a free independent spirit – I became a seagull flying high and free, following my own dreams and desires regardless of what others thought seagulls ought to do, just like *Jonathan Livingston Seagull* – one of S's favourite books.

As we researched further we began to sense that the wisdom that emerges through exploring suicidal processes is often relevant not only to the person who is suicidal but also to others who are connected to them. I have shared, with other members of my family, the idea of not needing to die in order to fly free – of finding creative ways to live our lives freely and ways to 'kill' or let go of the parts of ourselves that limit us. My niece has found it particularly helpful both in understanding more about why her father killed himself and in finding ways to live her own life more creatively.

Over the years there have been many times when I have asked myself 'Did that really happen or did I just dream it?' or wondered if I really was going mad. Being willing to open up to the deep dreaming that underlies our everyday experiences has taken me to some far-out places and some far-in ones too! The more often I am willing to explore these dreaming processes with curiosity and without judgement, the easier it becomes to drop the question of whether I am in a process of emergence or crisis and the richer and more creative my life has become. I often have a sense that the spirits of the dead are also happy that we are doing this work – I feel their presence strongly and there have been many synchronous signs and occurrences which have helped me to continue to explore this often taboo subject. Participants in our workshops often speak about how relieving it is just to be with others who share the experience of being bereaved by suicide and are willing to talk about it and engage with it creatively. Witnessing and being there for each other is a huge gift for those of us whose loved ones and colleagues have chosen, through suicide, not to be here with us.

I am grateful to all those courageous people – the living and the dead – who have accompanied me along the way, and I dedicate my continued exploration of creative living and dying to my brother, who I feel as close to now as I ever have and who I still miss very deeply.

Learning/discussion points:

- It is relieving to be with others who share the experience of being bereaved by suicide, to talk about it and engage with it creatively. Witnessing and being there for each other is a huge gift for those of us whose loved ones and colleagues have chosen, through suicide, not to be here with us.

- Pain and disturbance is not the whole story. Opening up to the deep dreaming that underlies our experiences of suicide with curiosity and without judgement makes it possible to move beyond questions of emergence or emergency and live richer, more creative lives.

- The wisdom that emerges through exploring suicidal processes can be relevant not only to the person who is suicidal but also to those around them. Asking 'What in my life wants to live more and what needs to "die" in order for this new life to flourish?' can also be powerful preventative medicine.

11

Pepe

Karen McDonald

Growing up I was very fortunate to belong to a large extended family. We lived on a deprived housing estate, something I was not aware of until I was older. Either we were all in the same position or my parents protected me from the deprivation. It was a happy upbringing, living with my parents and my brother, who is three years my junior. I was very close to my nana, Wee Robbie; she bore ten children: six sons and four daughters. They lived in a two-bedroom council flat; life must have been really hard for them. One child died aged 1 with reported measles; however, this would probably have been meningitis, with the knowledge of symptoms we are aware of in these times. I spent most days visiting my nana. All the children had grown up and got married, except one uncle, my uncle Peter – we called him Pepe (Peppy) – who stayed with my nana till she died in 1983, aged 75. Pepe was more like an older brother than an uncle when I was growing up. He was a stable factor in my life, full of fun, advice and torment. They were good times, lots of lovely memories. I remember a day when I was around 8 years old. The police came to my nana's door to inform her they had found a body and believed it to be my uncle. My nana told them there was no way it was him as he was at his work. She sent them away with a flea in their ear, informing them if her son was dead then she would know. The police explained that he had a National Insurance number in his possession and that is how they identified him as being her son. I was beside myself, believing them, but also clinging on to the hope that my nana's instinct was right. These were the days before mobile phones so we had to wait until he was due in from work. What a long day it was!

Right enough, my uncle came in from work at his usual time fit as a fiddle. It upset me for a while thinking what if that had been genuine. They brushed it off and got on with the day ahead, as only adults can do. Children are deeper and worry more. As time went on I forgot about it. As I grew up he was always there for me, I could talk to him about anything. He reluctantly gave me cigarettes when I had no money, and gave me my first vodka and lemonade. It was Pepe who took me out in as his brand new car for driving lessons when I was 17. We never as much had an argument but boy did we fight when I was driving. He persevered though, and I finally passed my test.

When my nana died, Pepe moved in with his partner and had children. We were still close but our lives moved on. I got married and had children. I enjoyed visiting him with my girls – he loved children and was always full of life. He was good to everyone. Always had a story to tell; he was a postman for many years and knew lots of people. Pepe became ill with lung cancer. He had an operation to remove his lung and recovered very well from this. When he was in hospital was a time that I couldn't be there for him; but I did visit him at home after the operation when he was up on his feet again. I was too scared. I didn't understand cancer and was scared of it. All I could think was he was going to die, and it brought back memories of that day the police came to the door when I was 8.

As always seems to happen in life, families have problems. Our family was no exception. There were ructions in the family over some of the younger members. I am not going to tell this story as it would be unfair to represent their feelings when they are not involved in this story. It caused a lot of bad feeling between their parents. When my own mother was ill also with lung cancer, it was a period of high expressed emotion for everyone. Life just didn't feel the same. I honestly think this was the time I actually grew up, not when I got married or had my children but when I had to deal with illness and death. It was at this time I decided to change career and study mental health nursing. On reflection, I thought I could maybe change the world at the time. I think it was more than that though: I think the main contributing factor was to make sure that people would be treated in the same way as I would want my family to be treated. This was around the time that Pepe got his five-year clear from cancer from his consultant. We had a family wedding around this time. This was the first time that the family had all been together in the same place apart from at funerals. Pepe spoke to everyone and made his peace. We had a post-mortem over previous problems and aired everything. I actually felt we would all get back to being the close family again; how wrong was I.

I received a phone call to say that I was to go to my aunt's as Pepe was dead. I had just pulled up to university for my lecture. It was a Friday morning, a day that I will never forget. I didn't go home, I went to the lecture. I guess I tried my nana thing: if he was dead I would know about it. During the lecture I sat thinking that this was really bad news and must be true. I had this sinking feeling that he must have committed suicide or had been murdered. My thoughts raced back to the wedding reception and it all fell into place. He wasn't making peace to get the family back together. He was planning his death and wanted us to feel better when the time came. I racked my brains thinking what the last thing we said to each other was. It came to me: it was I love you, and see you soon. This tormented me too as I began to doubt my ability to being a mental health nurse; I couldn't even read the signs that my uncle was in a dark place. I was in my first year and had no patient contact at this time. It was my theory period, no ward experience. The thought of being confronted by people who were feeling suicidal became so scary. How would I be able to help them? Perhaps I should just give up right now?

I drove down to my aunt's. All the family were there, just sitting looking at each other. They had already lost a sister and brother a month apart three years earlier, my mother and her brother. This was too much; suddenly they all looked so old and grief stricken. I had to get out of that room, it was awful. I didn't know how I felt. Anger was my first emotion. I learned he had gone into the woods near his house and hangede himself from a tree. I felt sick and was angry that he did not come and speak to me about how he was feeling. Angry at me for not recognising he was even contemplating this. What could be so bad in his life that would make him want to do that?

I was speaking to one of my friends who told me that it was a young council worker who found him. He had been clearing rubbish, a young lad in his early 20s. I was angry at that too, that poor lad coming across that situation; he would be scarred for life. The main reason I felt angry was my mother was dead and I needed her. It is always your mother who makes things right. I didn't speak to his partner as we hadn't met to make our peace at this time. I wanted to but like everything in life you put off all your todays until tomorrow as you feel like life is eternal.

I opened up the local evening news. On the second page there was a picture of them bringing Pepe out of the woods on a patient trolley. My heart stopped beating for a second – it was the most disgusting thing I had ever come across. I phoned up the editor of the paper screaming at him and his gutter press for being so insensitive towards our family by publishing that photo to sell papers. I have seen that many times before and never gave it a second thought. When it is your own flesh and blood, it hurts to the core to see these images spread over the newspapers. Sensationalism at its worst – I was so appalled. I didn't allow myself to grieve. I felt there were no tears in me, only anger. It wasn't until the day of his funeral that I became an absolute mess. It was during the service; they talked about his life and his untimely death. There was no mention of suicide, and I was asking myself why. Why is suicide such a taboo in church, even in these times? I wanted to stand up and ask why it wasn't mentioned: how were we all supposed to move on, when the way he died appeared irrelevant? Wouldn't it have been kinder for someone to say a few words on the subject of suicide? Help others by accepting suicide happens and sometimes this appears to be the only way for that person. I did not want the minister to condone it in any way; I just felt that it is part of a lot of families' lives and will always be there. Would it be so wrong to include this during this hour service?

Death is supposed to bring families together. I didn't want to lose sight of this fact. I tried to make it up with Pepe's partner but perhaps the funeral was not the best place. As the weeks went by it was still unresolved; I decided to just leave it at that. Another case of burying my head in the sand I suppose. It wasn't until my father died that we all managed to bury the hatchet and make our peace. We are not back to being the close family but have made up for all the right reasons. There are problems going on with other family members that will never be resolved. I have come to accept that this is life; it is not how you expect it to turn out, but take away some vital members of the family and it breaks down. I think my way of coping with it all is to concentrate on myself and my two daughters. Rightly or wrongly it is how I am coping at the moment.

I no longer torment myself with what I could have done to intervene to stop him from taking his own life. The simple answer is nothing. He left a letter apologising to the family with a simple 'Say to the family I am sorry.' That hurts too, the fact that he had the awareness to say sorry to the family but it was not enough of a protective factor to stop him doing it. I feel I have to respect this was his wish. At the time I felt it was a very selfish thing for him to do. Now I realise it must have been a very brave if not desperate thing to do. It is so final and the destruction left behind has been horrendous. It must have been meticulously planned in advance. It was not done on a whim. The missing piece for me was what was the final trigger that destined that time was right to do it? Another question in my mind that I know will never be answered.

Having experienced suicide in the family, I have had to become very aware of my feelings on the subject. I am in the privileged position to listen to people who have intentions of taking their own lives. My own personal awareness enables me to respect a person's feelings at this time however sticking to boundaries and exploring exactly how they feel and why they feel this is their only option at this time. I always ask why they feel that is their right to do such an act and ask how they think it would impact on their families if they did so. I have not actually experienced a patient having a successful suicide. I can only hope my interventions make them think of other options. Perhaps this comes from regretting having that opportunity to do the same for Pepe.

It has been three years since his death; it still feels like yesterday. I have not got over his death: I have learned a way of coping with it, living my life differently, but the sadness remains. I have contact with his family now which is comforting. It breaks my heart some days when his youngest daughter posts on Facebook that she wished her dad was here today to help her. She is the real tragedy in this story – to lose a father so young and in such tragic circumstances must be awful.

As they say, life is for the living so we must carry on in the best way we can. We are in this life for a short time so it is best to make the most of it whilst we are here. Whenever I read of a suicide in that local paper it brings it all back as if it was only yesterday. The one positive thing that came out of my outburst to the editor is they have never published another image like that again.

Living on the edge

Abigal Muchecheti

12

As a child, I always left to adults the grief of dead relations. I did not have the time to think about what it all meant. Most of the time my parents would go to the funeral and come back home. My religion gave me the other explanation, in which people die and the pure go to heaven while sinners go to hell and that was all I ever thought about at that point. I also knew I did not want my parents to die and leave my brother, sister and me alone. My aunt then passed away and upon agreement my cousin Susanna came to live with us. Susanna was a cheerful girl but from time to time she became a bit moody. I watched with interest at first thinking it was the age, becoming a teenager. And besides, she had lost a mother. Much as my mother accommodated her, obviously having lost her mother must have been painful. She would be happy to talk with all of us. We would help her with her homework and all seemed well.

From time to time Susanna visited her father and brothers who still lived in the family house. Her father had remarried and life had to go on for the rest of the family. When she was 16 Susanna fell in love. We all worried about her getting pregnant and talked to her about practising safe sex. Susanna went on all about 'I know what I am doing', like all the young teenagers say, but our fears were confirmed – she became pregnant. At 17 she was a mother. Everything seemed well. She was happy and got back to school. The family helped with looking after the baby and Susanna seemed less restless. She loved her daughter and was a proud mother. I adored them both. When I left home for university, I used to call home just to talk to my little niece. The family gave Susanna all the support they could. If we were worried about her behaviour before she got pregnant, now was the time when we should have really checked what was happening. She enjoyed being a mother, but then sometimes she would behave like she didn't care. She would leave home with friends and just not come back home. If asked she would be so upset, she would not talk to anybody. Sometimes she would simply lock herself in her room, not letting anyone talk to her. Sometimes she would not even eat. Then immediately after such behaviour she would be so happy and normal again.

We kind of got used to her moodiness. Whenever that was pointed out she would just laugh it off. I wanted an answer but she seemed to have none. She simply said it happened and she didn't know why. At the time we thought it was because she was a young mother so the effort the family gave was on helping with looking after Zora, her daughter. We assumed that her moodiness was due to the pressure of being a teenage mother. I tried to talk to her as one would do to a younger sister but I got the feeling she never recovered from the loss of her mother. Furthermore, she didn't really want to open up. I had to force her to talk to me which didn't help the situation. My mother tried to talk but she was tied up looking after Zora. I encouraged her to go out with friends or even have friends around, but she wanted to be left alone. As long as she was not physically ill, I thought she would snap out of her mood and be happy.

All of a sudden Susanna did snap out of her anger or whatever it was and she was different. She decided to go back to school and there was talk of moving abroad. I thought she was doing well and was proud of her. Then I moved to the UK from Zimbabwe. We spoke on the phone regularly and I enjoyed all the updates she gave me on Zora, her daughter. She seemed happy. Susanna even called to tell me next time I go back home she would be showing me her new boyfriend. I was pleased for her. It had been six years and Zora was going to school now. At 22 we thought Susanna was now in a better position to handle a relationship. Nine months later I was told she had a baby boy. I was happy and she was living with the boyfriend now. From what I heard, the boyfriend was the lazy type and there were constant rows. Whenever I asked about it, she would say it was not as bad as it seems. She was managing. There was no need for me to worry. All would be alright. I trusted her. In the past years she had been telling me everything, so I thought at the time.

One day out of the blue, I had a call from Martin, Susanna's brother. Susanna was seriously ill and was in hospital unconscious. I was beside myself with worry. I was confused and all sorts of things were going on in my mind. Martin did not at first mention the drug overdose that had knocked Susanna unconscious. Susanna had allegedly taken her five-month-old baby to her bedroom, made sure she was asleep, emptied the malaria tablets that were in the bathroom cabinet and went to sleep knowing she was not going to be alive when her baby woke up. She had just said to Martin, she was tired and was resting. Martin had come to see how she was doing and was about to go back when he thought he should check on her and leave a note to say goodbye. But when he got in the bedroom, which was not locked luckily, he found Susanna making some choking sound with foam around her mouth. He quickly checked on the baby, who seemed normal. He called Susanna and called the ambulance but unfortunately was turned away at the nearest hospital because they said she was dead. She was taken to the next one but it was too late. She never regained consciousness and a couple of hours later she was pronounced dead. There was no suicide note or anything that suggested she intended to commit suicide.

I was gutted. I didn't understand and at first thought Martin was going to call me back and say he had made a mistake, it was not Susanna. I was in denial. I just could not believe the girl I had grown so fond of over the years had just taken her life. *'Why Susanna, why? Why didn't you talk to me?'* I kept on asking myself. I didn't think she was the sort to just end life considering she had two kids including a five-month-old baby. Why did she not talk to me? It was unlike the Susanna I knew and I was angry with her. How could she shut us all out like that? What were we going to tell her kids?

I asked Martin what was happening. I wanted answers but he didn't know either. Martin thought I knew more than him about what was going on in Susanna's life. John, Susanna's boyfriend, had no idea what had gone wrong. He was at work at the time Susanna committed suicide, and the previous night they had not rowed. As far as John was concerned, the relationship had been doing well. I really wanted to find out what had happened to my cousin and why she had killed herself at 22. I felt useless. If I had been there for Susanna, she might not have taken her life. I had not been able to get to the bottom of her moods and maybe I should have encouraged her to seek advice. My mother had helped with Zora and maybe on her own with an unsympathetic husband Susanna might have found it hard to carry on. I kept on thinking of what could have gone wrong and tried so hard to read between the lines of all our previous conversations. Did I fail to pick out signs of depression? I felt guilty and blamed myself for not having seen it coming. Susanna seemed to have been living on the edge since losing her mother. Maybe the family should have done more. It was difficult to fathom. I had to come to terms with losing her but the hardest bit was the suicide. I had lost a friend, a young sister I had seen grow from being a young girl to a mother of two. We had laughed through some of life's challenges and cried together when things were tough. She was younger than me but we were close and I was going to miss her. From what I heard Susanna's mother had committed suicide. At the time it was hushed for Susanna's sake. My mother had thought it was not a good idea to mention or even talk about it. Nora, Susanna's mother, had poisoned herself.

Maybe if I had known, I would have treated Susanna differently. Still I had thought if someone was going to kill themselves, they would show real signs, something that would be quite obvious. I never thought it would be just the decision of the moment. I wondered what had made Susanna snap that day and just use the malaria tablets for such a dreadful thing. Martin thought, maybe Susanna never intended to kill herself but wanted her boyfriend John to pay more attention to her and the baby. As an explanation to the suicide, it made sense but the family would never know what made Susanna snap. John was of the opinion that if Susanna wanted to commit suicide it would have been immediately after she had given birth because she was finding coping with the baby a challenge. Five months later was unbelievable because she seemed to have been enjoying being a mother again.

I still think the family will never know what made Susanna commit suicide. She did not leave behind a suicide note and left us to accept she was gone and guessing the reasons she decided to end her life at 22. Having been appointed the guardian of Zora, I worry once again if she would do the same – end her life by committing suicide.

The other half

13

Jo Rhodes

From birth, the instinct to survive is a powerful one. Our lives focus around those things which ensure we thrive for as long as possible – eating, drinking, sleeping – with everything else being a wonderful bonus to our existence. That is what is so hard about suicide. To know that Adam no longer wanted to eat, drink or sleep in order to see the next day or the day after that was incredibly hard to deal with, and yet for years before his death I knew that he struggled with that very notion. He was always talking about what methods of suicide were the best – trains were too messy, drugs too prolonged, wrist slashing too unreliable. He was brought home by the police about a year before his death because they had found him sitting on the bridge over the A30, his belongings beside him. Later he said he was glad they had found him because it meant that he hadn't impacted his misery (and his very being) onto the lives of some poor innocents who were driving along the road and found themselves in the wrong place at the wrong time. Another time, he left me, then sent text messages all through the night threatening to commit suicide. I convinced him to come home and go to the doctors. He was placed under the care of the mental health team, diagnosed with OCD (obsessive compulsive disorder) and severe depression. He passed the time by etching marks into his arms with any blade he could find for about three weeks before the drugs kicked in and he went back to work.

Each crisis left me feeling more and more responsible for maintaining Adam's life as well as my own. I wouldn't leave my car at home with him in case he gassed himself, and the endless walks he would take himself off on would leave me sat at home waiting for the knock on the door. I knew that he would go through with it one day, in my heart. I suppose I just lived in hope that that day would never come.

On 8th May 2007 I finished work at 4 p.m. and drove home. I was five months pregnant, a new hope in our lives. The second scan exactly a week before had shown that we were expecting a healthy baby girl! After two miscarriages, I couldn't quite believe it was happening and we hadn't done anything in preparation for our new arrival. I was so tired. Every day was a struggle, not helped by Adam's illness.

I pulled into the drive to see the front door open, not an unusual occurrence if one of us was in. The television in the lounge was blaring out Sky Sports to an empty room. I continued my search through our home but it was strangely quiet. Then I remembered that Adam had a driving lesson booked! Ahh, mystery solved! So I got myself a cup of tea and idly sent Adam a text to see if he was OK. I heard a text alert from the garage, emanating through the internal door. I went over to the door and opened it. Behind the door and now directly in my eye line was my 28-year-old husband. He had a rope around his neck and was hanging from the rafters in the ceiling. There was a small trail of blood coming from the corner of his mouth, his lips were blue. His eyes looked down and behind him was the ladder he had taken his last step from. His phone bleeped from behind him.

I think I screamed but no one came. Maybe I didn't actually emit any noise. I dialled 999. The operator told me to cut Adam down, so I did. He landed on the floor with an enormous rush of air which scared me and made me jump backwards. His legs cracked as they took the dead weight of his torso; his head bounced off the concrete floor on impact and his eyes didn't move. Despite my conviction that my husband was definitely dead, the operator insisted I start CPR. I shuddered at the feel of his cold dead lips as I tried to fruitlessly blow air into a corpse. A corpse that was wearing the wedding ring I had given him seven and a half years before, whose hair I had cut only that weekend, who was wearing his smart work clothes and smelt of cigarettes.

The ambulance turned up, closely followed by a lot of police who filled the house. Adam was officially declared dead at about 4.45 p.m. I lit my first cigarette of the day under the uncertain watch of a young policeman who had been assigned to sit with me.

My first thought was that the wait was over. He had finally done it. I was relieved.

I rang my mum and she was there within what felt like seconds, closely followed by the rest of my family, all wearing shocked expressions and offering much needed support. I wasn't allowed to tell Adam's family and the police set off with addresses and contact names in order to break the news.

There was no note, nothing to explain why now, why this day. All he had in his pocket was the scan picture from a week before and an application for paternity leave that he hadn't completed.

I waited until the coroner took Adam's body away for the necessary post-mortem. He gave me Adam's wedding ring as they left, which I put on my necklace. There was a lot of clearing up to be done but, for now, I put my dog in the car, got the cats in and set off for my parent's house with my mum.

I rang the people I wanted to tell directly and then spent the evening with both families, pondering over the reason why, what would happen now, what to do next ... They were all trying to remember when they had last seen him and all I could see was his blue face staring towards the ground with that trickle of blood ...

At 2 a.m. I asked if I could go home. Though reluctant, my Dad drove me and slept on the sofa while I got into our bed. The dog curled up beside me and we slept for a fitful couple of hours before getting up to walk together around the town, waiting for the day to start. It was raining. I wanted to get away, to be on my own, but I couldn't. My baby was suddenly my only friend, the only thing that mattered. I wanted to be alone with her. She was the only one who had seen what I had seen, felt what I had felt. I felt scared, lonely and terribly sad.

May 9th, 2007 and life after Adam began. I was checked out by a midwife, rang the undertakers and got ready to make my statement to the police. What I wasn't expecting was the statement they would show me in return.

I had a day where I was still Adam's wife, I was still married to the man I loved and he was still very much in my heart. I spent most of it with my parents. I couldn't eat but smoked a lot. People sent me messages that I didn't reply to and left answer-phone messages that I listened to and vowed to call back. The usual things when you lose someone you love in such a sudden way. That was Wednesday.

It was the Thursday, May 10th that it all changed. I had to sign my statement and was offered another one to read that the police had taken from a woman who had worked with Adam.

She stated that they had been having an affair for three years. There had also been others but she had been a constant. The people Adam had worked with were under the impression that our marriage was over and his behaviour had caused some problems.

I swore. Then I drove home, hacked into the computer and found all the evidence of this other life, the way Adam had chosen to spend his time away from me. There were pictures of him in bed with other women, in their bed and ours. One photo showed this woman standing naked in front of our mantelpiece in the lounge, my and Adam's newly married faces captured forever in our wedding picture in the background. I took that picture down straight away.

When I tried to tell people, they didn't believe me. Not Adam. He was always so vocal about his disapproval of extra-marital affairs and the kind of people who got involved in them. He had often told me of ending friendships because people around him were cheating on those they purported to love. Yet it was him all along. That was why the friendships had ended – because of their dislike of his morals rather than the other way round. I felt so foolish.

So the news that we were in arrears with the mortgage, there was no money in the bank account, we owed £3,000 on a credit card that I wasn't even aware we had, and he had personal loans of £8,500 was just an added thing to deal with. We hadn't paid any council tax and so owed that, too. He had two mobile phones, each on a £45 a month contract and then he had been texting this other woman hundreds of times a day – over a hundred on the morning that he died alone. His bills were coming in at £250–£300 a month and I had trusted him to sort out the banking. Not only did I lose my trust that day, I lost my husband. I hated myself for being so naive, so gullible. I held my bump. Now, she was my daughter and mine alone. He had opted out. Adam had been dead less than 48 hours and I was already starting to leave him behind.

I didn't tell many people about the other side to Adam's life at first. I didn't want the truth to tint or discolour the funeral for me in any way, or to impact on their memories. I wanted to show those who thought otherwise that his marriage wasn't over, that he had duped them as much as he had me. We were all victims of his actions. But was it his behaviour that had made him ill, or was his illness a symptom of his behaviour? He had made us all victims and then bailed out, leaving us to fend for ourselves.

I held onto the idea that Adam was ill and that the affairs had been a way of proving to himself that he was a bad person. The doctor's report showed that he hadn't ever attended counselling sessions as he had told me, nor was he on medication any more. The man who had carried out all these acts wasn't the one I had spent so many happy times with, yet I could identify him as the one who had thrown all the furniture around on my birthday because he had forgotten to get me a card, or had thrown plates at me for being upset when I had miscarried our babies. I could see this was the person who would tell me I looked too fat to go out or would tell me we were too penniless to afford moisturiser or make-up yet still buy himself a new pair of expensive shoes. With new clarity, I could understand that Adam was ill, a behavioural illness that split him into two people, or maybe more. I was determined to mourn the man I had loved and had been happy with. That was what would get me through the funeral. After that, well we would have to wait and see.

The funeral was on the 23rd at the crematorium. In the morning, I went for a final view of Adam's body and left a note with him: 'All is forgiven. All is forgotten. Rest in Peace Now, X'. I had to forgive him, however fleetingly, just to get through the next few hours. Over 250 people came. It was the hottest day of the year so far. One woman cried loudly throughout from the back of the chapel. I wish she hadn't. I read 'Stop all the Clocks' by WH Auden. This poem said that Adam was not in a broken marriage: he was in one that, on my part at least, was still true and lasting right up until he died. Until death do us part …? Well death was here and now I had to play my part. The grieving widow, dressed in black and obviously pregnant who stood outside and shook hundreds of hands, accepted the kind words from those who knew and those who didn't. The hurt soul inside me wanted to run and hide but there was still the wake to get through. An afternoon of distant family getting drunk and expecting my attention when all I wanted was to be with my dog on the moor and walk. I wanted my space now, I felt as though I had been on public view too long, under scrutiny for any signs of behaviour that weren't appropriate or befitting a widow in her 20s. At last, the drinkers left the party. I sat on the balcony of the venue I had chosen for the wake – Adam's golf club – and smoked in the fading sunshine with those I trusted, that I was closest to. I was tired. It had been a long day and now it was over.

The day after the funeral was the worst of them all. There was nothing left to do. Adam's things had been sorted through almost immediately and were away in the loft or donated to charity shops. The house was starting to get clean and I could only wait to hear from the mortgage company as to whether they were going to let me stay in the property. I had nothing to do except grieve. For so many things. For Adam. For my marriage. For the father my daughter would never have. For the life I had thought was guaranteed but that had now gone. For the betrayal I felt, the huge amount of lies I had believed, for the amount of trust I had misplaced. The world was suddenly spinning around me and I was totally lost in the power of life and the situation I was in, the situation he had created by being too cowardly to face what he had done. I seesawed wildly between hating him and loving him, glad he wasn't there and missing him so much it felt like my heart would explode. Forgiveness was replaced by anger and then swung back again. I didn't understand why; why now, why that way, why us, why me? If he had needed me, I had been there. If he needed his space, I had left him alone for hours, only to now know he was on the phone to another woman or uploading pictures of them having sex in my house to Internet porn sites. When he had contracted glandular fever and been in bed for three weeks, I had gone out in the early hours of the morning for medicines to try and make him more comfortable, and I washed the bedding. He told me it was going round work. Of course it was, but so was he.

Then I would get out two mugs when I boiled the kettle, or pull a packet of his favourite biscuits out of the cupboard, and the grief would wash over me and take the anger with it.

I booked an emergency appointment with my doctor, who referred me for counselling. Within days, I was sat in front of a counsellor and told her everything from the last few weeks without shedding a single tear but also without looking up. The fear of being judged or in some way deemed responsible was always there, ever present in the back of my head, the fear that the person I was talking to would think it was my fault in some way – I should have got him medical treatment (though I thought he was receiving it), I should have left work early, I shouldn't have left him alone, I shouldn't have got pregnant and put the extra stress on my husband or that I was such a bad wife, it was only logical that he should cheat on me. I stuck to the facts, the points that couldn't be argued with. The truth that was such a fragile and delicate part of the whole mix and mess of lies and tragedy.

That was the day that I took my wedding ring off for the last time. My marriage really was over. He was dead. We had parted.

The inquest in November, two months after the birth of my beautiful daughter, found that Adam had taken his own life when not in his right mind. The 'other woman' was called but failed to show and I was relieved. It was done, over with, finished. Adam's sister was present and I think she found it hard to process. With hindsight, it was the last time I felt she was part of my life. That day signalled the start of the separation between me and Adam's family. I was trying desperately to see myself not as Adam's widow but as my daughter's mother. I felt the responsibility of being a good parent to my child incredibly keenly because I had lived with the result of an unsettled childhood and was also aware of the hereditary factors with mental illness. I remember Adam's mother saying that men don't cheat without reason, that there must have been a problem in the marriage and it was usually the wife's fault. It was at that point I realised they were looking for someone to blame and they couldn't blame themselves so they were starting to blame me.

I blame Adam. Fair and square. It was his actions, his choices, which led up to the moment that he committed suicide. There is only so long you can blame the unsettling childhood, the absent father, the bullying, the failure at work, the loss of self-respect. But there is always help if you look for it, there is always someone to talk to, and he was old enough to know better. I blame him. He was ill, but he knew he was ill. There was time to get help, to take the medication, to talk to the experts. He didn't and they were there.

That was May 2007, nearly five years ago. My daughter is now a wonderfully healthy four-year-old who loves school, aeroplanes, trains and princesses – not necessarily in that order! She has a daddy and she loves him. He is here for her and he loves her. She is aware that Mummy was married to someone else before she was born but she isn't interested. Should she ever be, then I have a box of things for her to look through – papers, stories he wrote, our wedding photos, and the cards from the funeral. But she is safe and I am proud to be her mother rather than a widow. If I am honest then I have to confess that most days I think of him in some small way, if only fleetingly. I can't help it – we were married for over seven years and his suicide has had a massive impact on my life now. It changed my personality and opened my eyes to a level of life I had been blissfully unaware of. I find myself distrusting those I love and fearing the worst. I still get very occasional flashbacks that wake me from my sleep where I am staring at Adam's cold blue face as it swings from the garage rafters in a diverse range of weathers and scenarios. But I also know how dark and scary life can be and I try to appreciate the beauty of the world around me as much as I can. I appreciate the colours of the flowers and the songs of the birds. I want to make friends now and be a part of life rather than hidden away and scared of it. Adam took my world but he gave me the freedom to find another one, a more wonderful one. If only he could have seen it, too.

Learning/discussion points:

- In my experience, the issue of guilt and where it should be placed for Adam's suicide was and is the single most destructive emotion with regards to continuing relationships among the remaining family groups. There was very little talk of it ever being with Adam himself and I think this is an issue that should be addressed as quickly as possible through counselling or consultation.

- I was incredibly fortunate in that my counsellor was excellent and supportive without passing judgement or opinion. I felt I could express even the most fleeting or unrefined emotion or conception to her without fear of judgement, and my relationship with her was very important when I was trying to work through the events surrounding Adam's suicide as well as the suicide itself.

- The notion that I would 'get over it' was one passed by me by a couple of doctors and it gives the impression that one day you will wake up and will feel completely 'normal' again – or at least feel as you did before the event. This is false, as I remember waking up hoping to find it all settled in my mind and then being dreadfully disappointed when it wasn't.

14

Gilly Graham

I had been working in an office with a friendly team for about 18 months and a man called D worked in the office next to mine. He was an architect; well educated, well travelled, well respected, he did not suffer fools gladly, had a great sense of humour, was a kind and generous man, a good cook, and was a conscientious worker. When I walked into the building each morning there was always a waft of D's expensive aftershave to greet me in the hallway. Before each morning got fully under way, there would be banter of some kind – D complaining that there was no cafetière in the kitchen as I'd broken it months before; D telling a colleague her hair looked nice with a cheeky smirk on his face knowing she was due to have it done; D asking what homemade cake a particular colleague had made for break time, knowing full well she didn't home bake. It was a fun place to be, even though in between times we had work to do. The banter nearly always involved D and we all accepted his jokes, and sometimes insults, in good humour.

Often in our free time, some of us would meet up for a drink or go for a walk and D was one of those who liked to be involved. As a bachelor, he had no one to get home for, except perhaps his cat. Sometimes he'd tell us that he was cooking a homemade soup that evening, made from vegetables he'd grown in his garden, and that we needn't bring lunch in the next day as there would be plenty for all.

This was probably the most amiable working relationship I had had with any group of people in my working career, but like most good things in life, they don't last forever. D was asked to attend a works meeting and was told that he was being offered voluntary redundancy and that he had until the following evening to accept. When he came into the office and told us we were stunned into silence as it didn't seem real. This kind, hard-working, articulate man, who we often referred to as the Oracle, was going to have to leave us and he was shattered by the news, as were we. It didn't seem real that he was leaving us, our little team, so abruptly.

The following morning, he had been locked out of his works computer and could therefore not complete any work. Silently, this six-foot, well-built man packed his belongings into cardboard boxes, loaded them into his car and left without saying goodbye. We could only imagine how he must be feeling: left out, abandoned, picked upon, dejected, worthless, to name just a possible few. He was, after all, a professional man and proud.

Several staff from the office tried to phone him, at his home and on his mobile, but got no response. We even tried to email. It was a couple of days before he responded to anyone's calls or emails to check he was OK and he sounded like a broken man. He was angry – after all, he had worked tirelessly for the company who discarded him like an old pair of slippers. Work wasn't just a job to D, it was a huge part of his life, along with the people he worked with and met whilst carrying out his duties.

Several weeks passed and we saw less and less of D, though he did keep in touch with the occasional text or email to us. The office didn't seem the same – it was missing something, or *someone*.

One Friday he emailed to see if we could meet for lunch, which we could, but he barely ate anything and looked as though he had lost quite a bit of weight. It was noticeable because he was what I would call 'well covered' and he loved his food. Just before he left, he asked if anyone wanted a walk at the weekend. I was the only one not doing anything so arranged to walk my dog with him near his house, on the Sunday.

On Sunday morning, it was raining heavily and as the time got closer to me having to leave my warm, cosy house I contemplated whether to cancel the walk but in the end I decided not to. He seemed back to his old self, cheery and chatty, when I arrived. D and I walked in the now light rain, and chatted about his redundancy, about how safe I thought my job was, or wasn't, and he said how he missed us all in the office. I told him we missed him too and that it wasn't the same without him there. Back at his house he made tea and the old D teased me about the amount of milk I had in my tea – 'Do you want half a cow in that?' he'd ask. We chatted about what things he could do now, for work or as an activity. He'd mentioned perhaps doing some voluntary work, or getting a small job to help pay his mortgage but something that would allow him time to do other things as well, like going swimming, or doing his gardening and any architect jobs that might come up.

When I left, he came out to the car to wave me off in the rain. Little did I know then that this would be the last time I ever saw D.

In the early hours of Tuesday morning D made the decision to end his life and hanged himself. We found out about it on the Wednesday morning and I was struggling to believe what I had heard. I'd been told in the morning and although I was very upset by it, I did not cry until I got in my car to come home after work that day.

It's true what they say about the five stages of grief. I was starting with the disbelief. I wanted to check for myself, to see if he was still breathing, albeit shallow and almost undetectable and even though he had probably been found 24 hours earlier. I wanted to ask if the people who found him had checked properly to see if he was still alive. It was an irrational thought, I know, but it didn't stop me thinking it. I also thought it couldn't be possible that he was dead because we had only been chatting on the Sunday and I never picked up on how bad he must have been feeling. He'd seemed fine to me but then maybe I wasn't looking hard enough. I wondered if he'd known then what he was going to do or whether he made a rash decision when he had been particularly down.

Then I tried to reason in my mind, perhaps even with God, that if I try to rewind my life a few days I can convince D that life is worth living; just let me be able to go back a couple of days. Again, it's completely irrational but something I tried so hard to do – to think myself back in time a couple of days, and talk to him a while longer to find out how he was really feeling, to spend longer with him so he knew for sure just how much people cared about him.

I think that is probably when the guilt kicked in. Why hadn't I realised that he would do this? Why didn't I stay longer that afternoon and chat about things in more depth. Why hadn't I been a good friend to him and made him feel that his life was worth so much more? Shortly after I'd felt the guilt, I felt the anger.

I was angry at the company for treating him so badly and making him feel that he had no other option than to end his life. I felt angry at myself and my colleagues for not doing more to notice how upset he had been. I also felt angry at D for wasting his beautiful opportunity at life when others I knew had lost theirs through no fault of their own. I'd lost a family member to leukaemia only a few months before and he would have given anything to still be around.

The hours and then days after D's death meant that the people I worked with and I were not very able to concentrate on our work, our thoughts constantly being on what had happened to our friend and colleague. In a way, it was good that we all got on so well as we were able to support each other. We talked about what we could have done for him to prevent it, how he must have been feeling; questioned why he didn't talk to someone about what he was intending, so they could have helped to change his mind. We chatted about the funny things he'd say to us. We were all aware that D had friends all over the world and that we were just a few of the many people he knew, but we have many happy memories of him, as I'm sure do all the other people he knew.

Thoughts of D filled my mind constantly over the next few days, and I know they did with other colleagues in the office. Even when I was starting to not think about him, I would be reminded by the smell of his aftershave when I walked past his office; by walking into the kitchen and remembering breaking the cafetière; someone mentioning one of the properties he'd been working on; something on the news about someone committing suicide; or seeing the little packet of forget-me-not seeds we'd been given at his funeral.

Over the coming months, the daily thoughts of what had happened with D became less impacting, enabling me to concentrate and focus on other things. But the one feeling I still, on occasions, feel towards him at times is the anger – for wasting the chance of life which some people don't get a choice in; for making me feel all those unhappy feelings; for being selfish to his family and friends by denying us the chance to say goodbye on mutual terms. I feel angry for him doing what he'd done, knowing that someone he knew well would find him and remember how he looked for the rest of their lives and that it would have a huge impact on them. I was also angry that he didn't leave a note explaining to all of us about why he took his own life and telling us that it wasn't our fault, that we'd been good friends but that he just couldn't cope with what life had for him anymore. It would have made things easier, knowing that he had known we were there for him but that there really was nothing we could have done to prevent it. It would have made things easier for a lot of people that he left behind, I'm sure. How dare someone you cared about make you feel so badly, that perhaps we were in part to blame for what they did. I think suicide is a really selfish thing to do, although I appreciate that people who attempt or succeed at suicide probably aren't thinking of others at the time, but this doesn't make it any easier to deal with or accept for those left behind to deal with it.

For me, one of the ways I can now cope with this is to not think too much about what happened. I understand that it may not be the right thing to do, but I think less and less about D because of what he did, and how little I feel he must have cared about the people who cared about him.

It saddens me that my happy memories of D have been clouded by the anger I still feel towards him for doing such a self-absorbed deed when I was in fact happy with my life. That he impacted upon my life in such a negative way that it in turn impacted on my life, affecting people I cared about who never even knew D. I was upset and wanted time alone to think about things when I should have been perhaps spending time with my family and friends, as I usually would have been. If he had died from a medical problem or been involved in a fatal accident, my happy memories of him would have remained intact and I would have been able to accept the death more easily although I would still have gone through the usual stages of grief.

However, his death in such tragic circumstances made me re-evaluate my own life. D had been a man who had travelled the world, had received a good education and had a wealth of friends and a successful career. As far as I know, he had realised his dreams. I, on the other hand, still had a dream which, up to now, was something I thought would only have a chance of being realised once I was retired, which was years away. Knowing how short and unpredictable life can be, I made a life-changing decision to try and realise my dream now, while it was still a possibility, and I think if D had not committed suicide I would not have had the courage to take the step to give up work and sell my house and chase my dream. I suppose in my mind, I am using my change in circumstances to try and convince myself that something good has come out of something so awful. D made the decision to end his life – I made the decision to grab mine with both hands, to make the most of the people I have around me and to try to make every day count.

Learning/discussion points:

- The anger side of my grief has now passed and I can now remember D with fondness and remember the joy he brought to so many people's lives. I now make more of an effort to treat everyone with the respect they deserve, no matter how bad a day I'm having, because I know that no matter how much someone may be smiling they might have their own demons that they're having to deal with.

- If people are in the position of making others redundant, please think about each person as an individual who has a life, a family and deserves to be treated with respect. Treat them how you would like to be treated yourself.

15

A lifetime changed in a moment

Neil Ritchie

All those of us who were fans of M*A*S*H will recall the iconic theme tune, 'Suicide is Painless'. I'm not sure that's even true for the suicide victim. We've had Jeremy Clarkson's offensive outburst claiming suicide victims are selfish. I don't think we can even begin to understand the pain a person is in that they consider death as the only way out of the dark place they find themselves in. Still, for every victim of suicide, there are people left behind picking up the pieces and ultimately bearing a burden of guilt for what they didn't do for the victim. My experiences have changed me and my view of suicide, but I've spoken with enough people who are firmly of the opinion that victims are merely cowards who can't or won't live up to their responsibilities and have taken the easy way out.

My story begins on 24th November 2003. It was just another day really, nothing exciting or interesting was in the offing. About 9.45 a.m., one of my close friends called me at work. This was fairly surprising as we didn't have that much cause to call during work hours. But the reason for the call was stunning. I'm amazed he was able to hold himself together on the phone. I'll put that down to shock. Our closest friend – we had all known each other for years, and went to Aberdeen FC games weekly together – hadn't turned up for work that morning. Colleagues were concerned and two went to his flat when they'd had no response to phone calls. On failing to gain entry, police were called. What my friend had called for was to say my closest friend whom I'd known for 24 years had been found dead in his flat.

It was a massive blow. Still, I was remarkably calm immediately afterwards. I phoned my mother-in-law to get her to ask my wife to call me immediately. I then called my mum. I remember it all so well after all these years. She started to talk about what she had on that day. I stopped her and told her I had bad news, and that she should sit down. The silence that followed my news seemed to go on for an eternity. Like any sudden death, the shock was palpable. I finally spoke to my wife, who was likewise stunned. I was too shocked to go into any detail at work, but managed to make my excuses and left.

My wife immediately left work to come and collect me. I was shattered by the news. Just the week before, my two friends and I had been enjoying some post-match beer in an Aberdeen bar. I think we thought that would go on forever. Within a week, that was cruelly taken away from me. I think from the outset, I wanted to believe that there was a natural cause for his death. No one wants to believe their friend was in such pain that suicide was the only release for them. Looking back, the first emotion was denial. Denial at his death for starters. 'You're kidding,' I said to my friend who gave me the news. What a stupid thing to say in retrospect. I didn't want to believe it, but it was true.

The next stage of denial was immediate. I wanted to believe the death was as a result of natural causes. I held on to that belief for almost two weeks until there was no denying it any more. Chatting with my other friend over a drink, we both reached the ultimate conclusion that the death was as a result of suicide. It was another shattering blow. Suicide was just a concept to me up to that point. Maybe I did think victims were selfish, and that it was the easy way out. That misconception was destroyed in one evening. Suddenly, I had up-close experience with suicide. My closest friend had purposefully taken his own life. My view on suicide was changed in an instant. I no longer saw it as an easy way out. I couldn't help dwelling on what my friend was thinking at the moment he started to take his own life. Oddly, I wasn't really thinking about how he was feeling. I was thinking about myself. It turned out the selfish one was me. Isn't that strange? Twenty-four years of friendship lost in that moment. Why did that happen to me? I wasn't thinking about my friend, I was thinking that I'd never develop another friendship like that. Upon reflection, it was probably at this point I considered myself to be a victim.

I think that this is often forgotten when a person commits suicide. People on the outside see a clear victim – the person that took their own life. But those closely affected are also victims – the ones that are left behind. As I say, I felt I had had a huge part of my life taken away from me, something I'd never be able to replace. That is true when anyone passes away. Those left behind dwell on what they have lost. When my dad died when I was 14, I knew I would miss him, and still wonder to this day what my life would have been like were he still with us. But at least natural deaths have a reason. There is often very little even medical personnel can do to prevent them. Death is just a natural part of living, and in time the pain diminished. But there is little guilt. When we know there is nothing that could have been done, it makes the healing process so much easier. Healing is hard though. We try to prepare ourselves when death is a possibility. On the evening before my dad died, he had been taken into intensive care, and my mum had been told that the following 24 hours were crucial. That night, I tried to come to terms with the possibility he would die. Even then, nothing could have prepared me from the awful reality of 36 hours later when my mum told myself and my brother that my dad was dead. Imagine what it's like when you are completely unprepared for it?

The immediate aftermath was hard to cope with. The selfishness continued on my part. I dreaded the thought of the funeral. I'd been to a few family funerals, but can anyone ever become 'used to' them? Being selfish, I'd probably prefer to give them all a miss. In my heart I've already said my goodbyes to the one taken away from me. In the time between the death and the funeral, it had become clear that it was a suicide. That only served to intensify the grief. I think it also made me feel resentful at what I'd lost. Feeling resentful and so selfish at a death were feelings I was completely unprepared for. I don't think that anyone who hasn't had first-hand experience of suicide is able to comprehend it. I don't think anyone can. Naturally, most people's experiences of death are those that are part of life: a loved one becomes ill, is old; death may be expected. But for someone to purposefully to end their life is something that could have been avoided, and I think it's only natural that anyone left behind does feel resentment, which is inexorably linked to selfishness. Part of me thought: why did my friend not want to be around us anymore? Of course, this is nothing compared to the thoughts and feeling of the suicide victim. But, it's natural I think. As much as we try to think of others, we need to be concerned with our own emotional and physical wellbeing. Feelings of resentment and selfishness act as a barrier, protecting us from facing what we're really feeling. It's a useful device for delaying fully facing the outcome of a suicide, and facing what we perceive to be our own failings.

Of course, what I'm getting at is guilt. As I've said, death is a natural part of life, and if we've made the most of our time with a loved one who passes away in the natural course of events, we can console ourselves with the thought that we made the most of our time with them. There's no guilt attached and in time the wound left by loss will diminish, leaving the warm memories behind. That's never the case with a suicide. During the many chats my friend and I had after the death of our closest friend, the central thread was what could we have done to prevent it? Going as far back as 2000, my other friend had said he had been at our friend's flat after we'd all had an evening out. After a few drinks, he admitted to having thoughts about attempting suicide. Thing is, he was always the life and soul of any gathering. Had we just laughed it off, thinking it was just beer talking, and that it was wildly out of character? There were concerns that he had financial trouble, but then what can you do if a friend denies there is a problem? That doesn't stop the guilt though. With the benefit of hindsight, should we have put two and two together? At what point do you stop believing there is nothing wrong with a person? You ask if anything is wrong, and if there is nothing concrete that suggests anything to the contrary, is there any other choice but to believe that?

In the summer of 2003, we were all away at a friend's stag do. On the Friday evening, my closest friend said he wanted to go back to the hotel we were all staying at. He seemed so down, but then we had had a few drinks and it seemed so easy to dismiss that. After I'd gone to bed, he'd gone back out and got in a taxi to the street he had lived in 30 years prior. He'd done the same to another house he'd lived in in England some years ago. In the midst of all that, we made no link, but it now seems obvious to me he was visiting all his former residences for the last time prior to taking his own life. That's a sure-fire recipe for guilt. I look back and wonder why we missed the obvious signs that something was drastically wrong in my friend's life. Is it because we don't want to believe that anyone close to us would feel such despair that suicide is the only option? Do we think that there is no way any of us would ever fail a friend if we thought they were in desperate need of help and support? It seems a reasonable reason for our lack of action.

In early 2003, my friends were on a whisky-tasting trip up to the Elgin area. My closest friend had left the group and was found a few hours later by police walking along the busy A96 road to Inverness. He had been drinking, and had no idea of where he was, and why he was there. Police advised that he'd been quite emotional. A clear cry for help? I think so, but a cry we failed to heed. On top of that, he'd seen a doctor about how he'd been feeling, but nothing seemed to come of that. Were we the only ones who had missed the warning signs? It seems not. Somehow, it's little comfort to me that a healthcare professional also missed potential signs that my friend was a suicide risk. Would it be wrong to hold some anger against that doctor? After all, they have extensive training. But a general practitioner's knowledge base is just that – general. Without a referral to a psychiatric unit, all that was done was to prescribe medication – unfortunately giving out the means to carry out a suicide. But I think such anger would be misplaced. It's myself I'd point the finger at. All involved probably feel they could have done more to help. As I say, all the signs were there, but we just ignored them. Had we recognised them, maybe we could have done so much more and could have pressed for a psychiatric referral. Perhaps there was a reluctance to confront the demon that is mental illness. I spoke about it with friends of my brother sometime later. They looked at each other and immediately considered the symptoms my friend had as being typical with manic depression. It seemed so obvious. The lows he went through were all there, but there were periods where he seemed happy and settled. My other friend was married in September 2003, and my closest friend seemed happy and content at the wedding, and gave no signs there was anything wrong. Maybe he'd become so skilled at hiding the truth from us that it was easy for us to put any dark thoughts about his mental health well to the back of the mind. Perhaps because there is a general lack of understanding of mental illness and an ongoing stigmatising of the subject that we subconsciously ignored it. Whatever the reasons for it, the consequences of our inaction were tragic.

We all live in our own little world, and as time has gone by, we cocoon ourselves to the point where we are blind to everything that is going on around us. Maybe we don't want the hassle. Maybe we see the problems of others as just that – their problem. Hindsight is a brilliant thing, and it would be wonderful if we had its benefits at the outset. It's up to all of us to keep questioning and doing our utmost to help those who need it. We're all reluctant to get involved, and those in need are often resistant to the idea that they need help. The lesson I learned was don't give up. Just because a person doesn't admit they need help, it doesn't mean they shouldn't get help.

To this day, I think of my friend. My wife and I gave our firstborn son my friend's name as his middle name as a simple way of remembering him. It's one regret that I have that he didn't live to see my children. Although he never gave any outward signs of being happy around children, I knew him enough to know that he'd have been brilliant with them. It's so sad that he was given so little to be positive about. It's sad that he didn't realise how much loved he was by family and friends. But what saddens me most is that I didn't know how to help him when he needed my help the most.

Learning/discussion points:

- GPs (general practitioners) need to examine all referrals in relation to mental health.
- Look out for your friends, and take the time to be more understanding.
- Don't hold back on talking – it could save a life.

16

Self-portrait

Lost Soul

Moi lost soul reflections of my past ...

Abandoned at birth, I was truly blessed, extremely privileged to be adopted by the most beautiful couple, my Mummy and Daddy. They gave me the greatest gift of all: pure, innocent, unconditional love. They built an invisible fortress, cocooning, protecting me, for one can climb walls. This little girl inside me still yearns and pines for their priceless love, for it never leaves me; there is no word that can express the depths of my deep inner pain's sorrows.

I was an innocent 7-year-old child surrounded with an abundance of love when the darkness of self-destruction reared its vile despicable forces within me. I found it a pleasure to consume perfume. Why? I can only thank god that my parents were never to discover this; it would have destroyed them, and they did not deserve this. It was my dark secret.

I was 9 years old when I was injected by the powerful, addictive drug, sex. Unknown to me it will change my destiny forever and ultimately be my self-destruction.

Hey, you had better sit down as I reveal a wee bit of moi for I flew into tomorrow before tomorrow hit me. I was the tornado and time could not wait for moi. Blink and you'd missed moi! I could fly, for no one could clip my wings; not even my doomed marriages could shackle moi, for I was a free spirit. Oh why did everyone want a piece of moi? I was never on the stock market. It is impossible to condense all my journeys into a small space ... I guess there may be another book inside moi?

I loved and lived the life, no boundaries, just a never-ending roller-coaster of the unknown. Alas tragic events along life's journeys eat away at my very heart and soul like a parasite. A personal tragedy I lost moi and ultimately my identity. As is now, a lost soul.

This corrupt system has not only given me a national insurance number but a label 'The Personality Disorder 301'. Guess I should thank those 'above' that promote my emotions for their selfish gains, the gold diggers. For dollars mean nothing, oh I've wiped my backside on them many times, for moi. People are priceless.

Whilst contributing to this book, I have yet endured six bereavements in such a small space. I was on the edge of the ultimate inner peace, yet a stranger had cast out a lifeline to moi, like an angler to catch fish. This good Samaritan unbeknown to herself saved moi. Who is this good Samaritan I hear you ask? It is a beautiful, precious, priceless Lady, an editor of this book! For she gave moi a purpose in life and priceless lady you are embedded in moi heart. God bless you, priceless lady.

I wonder when the next chapter of my existence will arise and wash over moi like the crashing of waves or will I be rinsed and drown?

Watch this space ...

I wish to dedicate this small piece of moi in ink to my soulmate, whom I shall call 'my white rose', for I was with him before the night he died. I am still awaiting the dreaded inquest. 31.5.72 – 27.3.2012. I know you are waiting for moi, as you always did in life. I love you white rose from your panda.

Lost Soul

Born in 1961 to a woman with deep psychological difficulties, a paranoid schizophrenic, and a man whose life revolved around alcohol. Adopted into such a loving and caring family at the ripe old age of 6 weeks only for my 'parents' (although not biological, I regarded them as my parents) to lose their lives whilst I was in my teens. There was only one, chaotic outcome. This is my story.

Who wants to live forever? (Freddie Mercury – Queen)

I wish to reach out with my heart and dedicate my personal chapter for my child and all the lost souls in the world. (Written by a lost soul)

I have not revealed any of the persons identified in my chapter, purely for the utmost respect I have for them. Some of them were unable to defend themselves in life and now in death.

I wish to express my sincere gratitude to all the very special people who have supported me in writing this chapter, for without them it would not have been possible.

They have all chewed me up and spat me out like poison. They took what little spark I had, they drained me of every ounce within, they stole my very identity as well as my mind.

I take yet another look through my mirror and I keep asking myself 'What am I?' and 'Who am I?' Tears of utter despair flow like a river flowing freely down my face. Everyone who knows me, even the mental health services, call me panda eyes. I guess it's all this so-called waterproof mascara and eyeliner I use? My face is stained and black like the depths of darkness in my mind. It's like a never-ending emptiness deep in the pit of my stomach. I am dead inside, yet I still breathe? I can only describe myself as an entity. I draw back my curtain and peer through my window to the world outside. The traffic is flowing; it is very busy in the outside jungle. I see people running, walking, getting on with their lives, in their own normal world. It must be rush hour? I have lost all sense of time and the days all seem to roll into one. You see, I exist in my own world. I don't want to be part of this mad, corrupt system. I have created my own safe haven and have decided to isolate myself. I am frightened of life; however, I do not fear death.

Yes my world is different and I am different. I am nothing special. I really don't know what I am now. I recall I was once a person, I think? Well, I have a beautiful, sentimental collection of photo albums which I sometimes look at and I see what was myself when I had a life and an identity. It can't be a dream, because these photo albums are real. You see when we are all born, those above us, the corrupt system, authorities and government gave us all a National Insurance number. What is all that about? Then you're just a number. And now I'm a label, I am a personality disorder 301.

The system stole my identity a long time ago. Now I feel as though I have no identity to relate to; the system calls this de-personalisation, yet another label! The system does not like my behaviour because I have chosen to isolate myself, and I cannot understand why. I don't cause anyone any harm, am I not allowed my freedom of choice? How wrong they are. Man from all cultures and countries has had to fight for freedom for centuries; maybe they don't perceive me as normal? What is normal anyway? I gave up on that question years ago.

The system always gets you, you can run but you can never hide. This is not a mere exaggeration to feel it is a violation of my basic human rights. I just feel the system wants to control you. Why would somebody want to control you? So many questions in my mind. I reach out for my electric knife and slowly slice into my wrists; the pain I feel is pleasure, a release from my existence. My warm blood oozes and flows like the rivers of Babylon. I feel my inner urge is to escape; it's intense and overpowering. I reach for my stash of medication. They slide down my throat with ease, I don't count them, there is no need. I can only express this as a climax, not of a sexual nature – it's a different level.

It is the ultimate freedom, like the birds in the sky, a final release from a tormented broken soul and mind. Darkness falls upon me. I am abruptly awoken by a cruel nurse who demands a water sample. I can't move let alone think, yet they're demanding me to give a water sample! I am threatened by being catheterised if I don't obey. Yep, I'm back in this institution again, hospital. I wish I could call it my second home, but alas this is no home. It's become like a factory, one in, one out. They have even tagged me again, yet another number. I didn't realise I was a criminal? I see the derogative looks from certain members of the medical profession; I feel like something you remove from the soles of your shoes, I am dirt.

This isn't the first time, you see. They perceive you as an attention seeker. Trust me; I can think of many more ways to attract attention. I am not doing this to be in the Guinness Book of Records – it is not a competition either, it's me. I do not want sympathy, just inner peace. I feel that the need to punish myself is justified. Everyone pays the price, and I am willing to pay mine.

I, like so many, am very misunderstood. These institutions are now like the back of my hand. I recognise the genuine staff from those that are there for the money. I am witness to this through my own experiences and that of my friends. The need to escape to my safe haven is desperate, yet I am detained like a criminal. They bring the 'feds' in, why? I wouldn't hurt anyone, only myself. I have endured many treatments in these institutions: the bitter charcoal, endless drugs that cabbage you, then you're swept under the carpet. I can recall waking up with my top ripped off, naked. I have politely asked staff if I may go out for a smoke, then been threatened with being put on a section. I have been threatened with a pair of scissors that they will chop my hair off if I do not obey them. The 24-hour suicide watch is a joke, one of which I have endured. They have the power to control you, and you see they cover up to protect themselves. Yes I have witnessed this and so have my friends. Nothing shocks me anymore; they also label me as a self-harmer. But I am not. I punish myself; I need to escape from my inner demons. I am a hopeless sinner and I deserve punishment. I have tried in sheer frustration and desperation to commit suicide, yet I am still here. I have lost count of my attempts, but then I've never kept a diary. I've set fire to my hair, only to have someone extinguish the very flames. I have crept out into the darkness of night and laid myself down on very busy main roads and tram lines and yet they still get me. I have taken countless overdoses, it's like my body refuses to surrender. Shame on my very soul: I even stole my friend's meds in sheer desperation and I rammed them down my throat.

In the darkness of night, I lay down in the middle of a very busy road, darkness enveloped me. I am aware of something over my face and I try in vain to tear it off, yet I am too weak. Blank. I can hear noises, machines. I feel so confused, fear, I try to scream, but nothing comes out. Blank. Where am I? I have tubes within my body; I feel confused and weak. Please help me! What is this hellhole? They have stolen my mind. To this very day, I cannot recall how I got in that hellhole. Again, I found myself in a ward, I feel dead, shouldn't this feel peaceful?

I tried to look around yet I can't see. I wake medical staff, doctors and nurses. Total disorientation. How long have I been here? I am told by a doctor I have been in the High Dependency Ward. My eyes are glazed, yet I see such sadness: I am amongst poor souls that are suffering, clinging onto life for they fear death. I am overwhelmed, consumed with such inner shame and guilt that my tears are uncontrollable. These poor souls do not deserve to suffer. Please forgive my selfish soul and let me die. I cannot bear to see suffering.

On many occasions I have found myself in the custody of 'feds'. The 'feds' say I am a danger to myself, yet surprisingly the 'feds' have actually treated me better than certain medical staff have. Whilst in custody, they have had to escort me to the institutions; however, they have never cuffed me, nor treated me like a criminal. They have stayed with me whilst I have seen numerous shrinks. Certain 'feds' have witnessed this and told me that they felt shocked and disgusted how I was treated, and have taken me back into custody. I find it so very disturbing and sad that there is stigma that still exists in these institutions. One can see a broken leg but not a broken soul, heart and mind.

Through my journeys through this crazy system, I have met such beautiful people; I don't see them as labels, nobody should be labelled! I see beyond this and throughout the years we have developed such deep bonds of love and trust, we can all relate to each other. We have all been lost in the system; we all feel that one has to go through certain experiences to comprehend them. We do not like the 'textbook' doctors who tell us how we feel. Although it doesn't seem as though I have a good thing to say about the medical profession, I have also met some very beautiful, devoted, compassionate, professional medical staff on all levels from top consultants, mind rapists, nurses, advocates that have never judged me and have listened to me. Indeed they have gone out of their way for me. I will never understand why I deserve this? These people are all embedded in my heart and no one can steal the genuine love I have for them. The true beautiful lost souls I have met, we are not just as friends, nor family, we are as one. We are all as faithful as the morning sunrise.

The impact of suicide is the most disturbing of my chapters. Just recalling these nightmare memories tears me up and rips my very heart out. There is no word that can describe or express my very tormented, guilty emotions. It is the dark side, it deeply disturbs me. It affects me physically like a cancer that eats away at my very soul; even writing this down, I am physically sick, tears of failure flow uncontrollably. My mind has tried to bury these nightmares, especially the first one. But now I will reveal and resurrect the dark side … I found my child, my whole world, barely breathing, the colour of death on the floor. Something inside me told me time was running out rapidly. I had to get a grip of myself. Was this instinct? I could not let my beautiful fragile baby go. It's not their time, please help!! The paramedics are with her and won't let me in the bedroom. We are in an ambulance racing against time itself. The ambulance abruptly stops and my baby's heart has given in. Panic. I want to die. Please don't go! Children's hospital, too much chaos and confusion. Where is my baby? They won't let me be with her. Questions are thrown at me, what is my religion? A strange man appears at my side and I see this dog collar. A doctor sits with me and informs me they have had to phone Guy's Hospital, the very hospital my baby was born in. The toxic unit at the hospital had to help save my baby's life. My baby is on life support and I am dead too. It is not real and I fail to recall much more. I don't know how many days went by before I even saw her, but thank God, miracles do happen as she survived against all odds. I break down. My beautiful 10-year-old daughter is alive, they saved her. I was never to enter that bedroom again; please forgive me that I can no longer write about this nightmare, it has just wiped me out.

Unbeknown to myself, more darkness was to unfold. Whilst I lived in London, I met a very outgoing and vibrant strong character. His personality and wit shone. He made me laugh, we became very close, we shared such beautiful times together. Time soon passes by and eventually he was to move to Leeds. We always kept in touch with each other and I often went to see him, yet, I saw and sensed that something within him was changing. I tried to talk to him and he told me that he despised the system and shame on me, in that time of my life, I didn't understand him. All I could see was my friend, this strong character deteriorating and ebbing away with my very eyes. It was as if something was sucking away from his very life and soul like a parasite. He became withdrawn and isolated himself from the world. A recluse. I now know, reflecting back, he gave up the will to live. It was to be the first time I found a dead body. He was 33 years old, R.I.P. my brother. I feel guilty that I failed you, for I did not see what I see now. I was young and blind. Please forgive me? It's not the same but I still have a photo of him that I treasure.

I have been down these corridors of this institution more than I would have desired. I can feel the echoes of despair and pain, it's everywhere. There's no escaping the vibes. Now if I were to write about all the lost souls that have finally found their inner peace through suicide, my chapter would be the size of a book, but I can reveal some of this sadness. My friends and I were to meet a very disturbed, lonely lost soul. There were always pools of blood on the floor, wherever he was. His poor arms resemble that of a slaughter animal. Yet, deep inside, he was such a mischievous, lovable man, and beyond his shell, he emerged and we all shared so much together in such a small space of time. The staff put him on a section, yet he walked out free as a bird and was to set himself on fire to never return. There were no questions asked, it was as though he never existed. I guess he was just another statistic to this despicable system. We still to this very day, my friends and I, talk about him and he left us a priceless gift. He turned our tears into smiles. Goodnight and God bless, darling. Yet another lost soul came into our lives. This beautiful mind had endured too much pain and losses through his life, yet we all bonded as if we had known each other for a lifetime. He was such a character, always one step ahead. He really brought so much joy into our hearts with his outgoing antics. I will never forget his kisses, he had so much love he was busting. He particularly took to my precious best friend and would do anything for him. He gifted him his personal tobacco tin, and that tin still exists to this day in my best friend's pocket. This wonderful character felt he was not receiving the quality of care he so desperately needed. He spoke to a certain member of staff and felt rejected. So in frustration, he discharged himself early and took a fatal overdose of drugs. My friends asked certain members of staff when his funeral would be but were never to be told. So many questions came into our minds: why did certain professional members of the medical staff not see he was unstable? Yet let him discharge himself early? Why did they not listen to him? And why were we not allowed to pay our respects at his funeral? Thirty-nine years old. Another tragedy. God bless him. I was about 14 years old when this rebel with a beautiful heart entered my heart and life. He was to become part of me and my life, he always called me his 'blondie'. We ran away, laughed, cried, fought, made love in public whilst the 'feds' watched us. We were not ashamed of our love. We went to court to defend our love; I did not know love was a crime? Our love was unconditional, no matter where my journeys took me, he was never a breath away. He was always trying to protect me from other men, predators. Trust me, he was always climbing through windows to get me, no matter where I was. He once brought me a white wedding gown, knowing that I would only wear black. I knew it was a hint, it made me laugh and cry. That dress was never to be worn. When I and my baby had to escape back from the Old Smoke, to the safety of my parents, he was waiting for me and moved in with me yet again. I guess he never ever left me. I was not to know it would be his twilight years. He chose to spend them with me. We knew each other inside out and he shared his suffering with me, we held each other, I looked into his eyes and soul and I was frightened. Trust me, I was desperate and I tried every avenue to get him the help he so desperately needed and deserved. I failed him. That destroys me; the system failed him and his so-called family have failed him all his life.

For the first time in my life, my beautiful rebel left me. He could not take any more, the rejection from his own family, the vultures, scavengers, and took a massive fatal overdose of drugs and alcohol. He was 40 years old. I only wish we had done it together. For when he died, a part of me died. His cruel mother had the lid of his coffin sealed deliberately so I could not be with him. She never even went to his funeral. I will never know to this day how she can sleep at night? Unbeknown to me, he had some years ago a legal will done and it was to me he left the majority. I was shocked and numb with grief. It meant nothing to me so I gave all the thousands away. All I wanted was him back. I was hurt and very angry and I ripped up all his photos; it was too painful for my heart. He also wrote me personal suicide letters, which I will take to the grave with me. Please forgive me 'cos I can never forgive myself, I have failed you my beautiful rebel.

We crammed and shared a lifetime of love together. My only comfort is that he is at peace and I can't wait to be with him. I know he will be there for me as he was in life. My love for you, rebel, will never die. They say time softens the blow, I say garbage. I have taught myself to put on a brave face to the world, but inside I am the walking dead. Every year I put on my calendar all my loved ones' birthdays that have now found inner peace and every year that passes, I have less birthday cards and gifts to give. I survived my falls, but it was not my goal and so many of my very close friends have also survived their serious attempts at suicide. Many years ago in the institution I met beautiful blue eyes. I looked deep into his eyes and I saw fear. He was very frightened and lost in the system and desperate to escape. He put a sword through his very stomach, which resulted in a life-saving operation, yet the fear remained in his beautiful blue eyes. He tried to hang himself, then found himself being punished. He was incarcerated within a small unit. Amongst very deeply disturbed minds, that will never see the outside world again, my friends and I visited these secure units; they appear very beautiful on the outside, but believe me, inside they tell a different story. Beautiful blue eyes was punished for suffering like so many lost souls I know. He is now back where he belongs, with his beautiful wife. For we, to this very day, are still very close and we have never lost contact. I do know of a man whom I shall refer to as a very tormented and confused soul with poor burnt hands. He committed suicide within a small unit, how can that be possible?

Years ago, whilst in an institution, I met a man who was and still is very self-destructive. God only knows how he is still here today from what he has endured. He's even had the doctors baffled. He's such a character, he makes me laugh. But inside, my heart bleeds for him. It was only the other week I met another lost soul and he revealed his inner pains to me. I will never understand how certain people in the past rejected him? And through his past, he sought comfort through garbage (smack); yet another beautiful precious soul on the road to self-destruction. I cried rivers for this man. I cannot bear to see any more pain, too many beautiful souls destroying themselves. Slow, painful suicide? The list of the lost souls is endless. There is a great deal of debate on suicide and I respect everyone's opinions. I have been told it's a coward's way out, yet I believe it is far more deep and complex and not to be judged.

Another night falls down upon my selfish soul; my mind is racing with guilt, torture and failure. Trust me I'm no good. I look in the mirror and I disgust myself, I do not like what I see. How can anyone love something like me? I despise myself. No matter what I do, I always end up hurting and failing the very people I love. I can never forgive myself; I truly wish I was dead. But the love I have in my heart for my precious child is infinite like the universe. And I have so much pure love in my heart for so many special people I have met through my journeys. If I were to write all of these people down, it would resemble a telephone directory. But I know these wonderful precious people know who they are. From an amazing consultant 'shrink' who wrote about me. Certain beautiful people from the substance misuse services and mental health services, the amazing advocates, two amazing charities, two beautiful female GPs and my true genuine beautiful friends, it's endless.

Now I've been robbed, raped, violated, but no one can steal my love! I am not educated through the system but I am a student of life. The more I discover, the less I understand? Hey, I forgot to mention, I do have a degree and master's at that, yep. I have a degree in self-destruction.

Regrets: Too many to mention. But I regret not being a better mother, a better person, and I wish I could have done more for my friends.

Desires: It's not God's beautiful world I don't love, it's this corrupt system I despise. Inner peace? But most of all, for my child to have a beautiful life, for she deserves it.

THINKING SUICIDE

My father's war **17**

Sid Prise

I've taken after my father in many ways: a love of literature and history, a passion for social justice, and a spirituality that has helped me through many hard times. More detrimentally, though, I've taken after my father's mental illness: schizophrenia coupled with bipolar disorder, characterized by auditory hallucinations, paranoia, and frequent bouts of suicidal ideation. In my early thirties, when I lived with him again after years of living on my own, our codependency culminated in a suicide pact we quite nearly executed. I measure my life's beginning, and the beginning of my recovery, from the moment I survived that bleakest point.

My father believed himself a very important man, always on the verge of being let into an 'inner circle' called 'the bourgeoisie', who made the decisions that ran the world. Throughout my childhood he often had to go away to hospitals, when the conspiracy became too much and he feared that he had failed his 'tests', and would be rewarded not with inclusion in the inner circle, but with assassination. He believed this was going to happen until his dying day.

Human society is nothing if not severely delusional, even psychotic, and all signs seem to indicate that our civilization is headed on a course to suicide. Society is rife with conspiracies, of powerful interests to sell you things, to get you to join a religion or vote a certain way, to make you think war against people on the other side of the world will make you safe. My father felt society's madness as few others I've met. This is an essential quality of the schizophrenic person: a perception of the madness all around you that gets translated by your own mind into delusions of persecution and imminent death.

My father's final crisis, before he was hospitalized permanently and died within a year, was precipitated by the approach of Hurricane Katrina. He was in the same hospital I had been in some weeks before, when I was dealing with suicidal depression following several months of homelessness at my father's side. In the week before Katrina hit, he had been warning everybody that the people of New Orleans should be evacuated at the government's expense. But no one heeded his advice in the hospital, and in his mind, the 'powers that be' who were always listening to him were also refusing to address the catastrophe he foresaw.

By the time Katrina arrived, we'd been thrown out by the last of several friends who'd been allowing us to stay with them. The week of the homelessness of hundreds of thousands of people, slowly dying in America's oldest city, became the backdrop for our final days, together in a transient hotel with a bed, a chair, and a TV blaring news of Katrina all day and night. It seemed obvious we had come to our end. My father had driven away nearly all my friends and his with his demands for money and favors. And I, the picture of the dutiful son (a picture he painted and for which I proudly modeled), had stayed by him through it all. His last friend.

There is a conspiracy against the poor. It is called capitalism, and to view it as such is, I think, the only sane way to understand the world. What is insane is to believe the conspiracy to be directed specifically against *you*. My father had made this schizophrenic connection, and was convinced the 'inner circle' was intent on his murder. Slowly or quickly was the only question. Should he die now, with a roof still over his head, when he still had running water and a bed? Or should he try to hang on for another week, or another month, or another year, and end up freezing to death, sleeping on some park bench?

The homeless in America are treated like cockroaches: who mourns for a dead one? We wanted to rent a refrigerator from the hotel for twenty-five dollars, but because my father dared to argue with them, we were refused the fridge even though we had the money. This meant that the insulin for Dad's diabetes would go bad in a few days, and there was nothing we could do about it. Without his insulin, my father would likely be dead within a week. He thought the most honorable course of action would be to keep shooting up with the bad insulin until nature took its course. I cried for the next 20 hours, begging him not to kill himself this way – telling him there were other options, that maybe we could go to a hospital and stay there until a social worker could find us a place. But he would have none of it, for the question remained: if not now, then when? The conspiracy had driven us to this desperation. Why would it ever stop, if it hadn't stopped yet? Life like this wasn't worth living.

I shared his train of thought. Without Dad, I'd have nothing. He said he did not want me around for his death, so I thought I'd go to a different hotel, get a bottle of whiskey and a sharp pocket knife, and end my life, too.

'Take the insulin with me, son,' he said then. 'We should not die apart.'

For the next 20 minutes I thought about it. This, here, now, would be my end. This little piss-yellow, stucco-walled room, not ten by twenty feet, alive with cockroaches and a blaring television showing the death of a city, would be the last room I'd ever see. Everything I'd ever done, all the books I'd written, all my struggles against the evils of my life, all the friends and lovers I'd known: now none of it would be known. Not even my family would know what happened to Dad and me, for he'd driven them away too, over the last weeks and months. I would die here with my father, and that would be how it all ended.

Then something inside me revolted against this! I felt as if a voice was telling me that this story *had to be told.* That if I did not tell it, it would fade into oblivion, right along with my father and me. I called the only two friends I had left, George and Miguel, the only friends Dad had not yet driven away. I incoherently explained my situation, and they got together to help me. George demanded I have my father committed. He and his wife, Michele, took me out to eat, and I kept going over my long-held objections to involuntary incarceration, and my feeling that the dignity of life was far more important than its indefinite duration. In other words, didn't my father have a right to kill himself? George said no. Finally I went back with them to the hotel, with the intention of convincing Dad to commit himself, or if I couldn't, of forcing the commitment in my name. Luckily, he went voluntarily.

With George storing our stuff in his garage, I crashed for the next several months on Miguel's sofa. He and I became closer than ever during those months, and I began writing my fantasy series, 'Twilight of the Gods', which is still in progress. In the final chapter of the yet-unfinished final book of that series, the elfin heroine Aurelia is old and has lost most of her friends to old age or war, and even the Gods have had to leave the universe. There is no one to pray to anymore, no afterlife to look forward to. Aurelia is weeping over the memory of her love of loves, Graaf the Orc Bard, who has killed the Evil God of his mostly evil race by weaving a Song of Death around Him, thereby killing himself, the weaver, too. Aurelia knows she'll never hear his music, feel his great arms around her, kiss him or love him in the flesh, ever, ever again. Yet she hears his song on the winds, played on his magical balalaika, and she realizes that, even without a heaven, even without a Father God or a Mother Goddess to save his soul, a part of Graaf would live forever in her heart.

Reading this passage to Dad as he lay in his hospital bed was my saying goodbye to him, and he wept. I'd written many stories over the years of living with him, and he'd delighted in listening and offering his critique. But this time, the last time I ever read to him, he simply wept, and told me he loved me.

I sometimes wonder whether I should have left him to die as he'd wanted, making his last stand, rather than living the last year of his life in a nursing home. He was tortured by fears of assassination all through that final year. When I visited him, he would tell me to hush while he listened for gunshots in the hallway outside his room, gunshots which he heard and demanded I hear too. His legs gave out on him for reasons his doctors could not determine, and he never walked again. He died sitting in a bed of his own excrement, believing someone had dissolved poison pills in his water.

Was this the fulfillment of his prophesy, that 'the conspiracy' would persecute him until he had absolutely nothing left? Would he not have retained more dignity if he'd died by his own hand a year before, when he still had a measure of independence and control over his life?

Sometimes I think the only way to have real control over one's life is to control when and how it ends. But I'm so glad I didn't end it. My life is beautiful now. I live in a collective house with good friends, with whom I share political and spiritual camaraderie. I've written my best books thus far. And I'm in love with a beautiful, kind, and loving woman, Kathy, a fellow Mad and fellow Queer writer and urban homesteader, whom I married in 2008. My life *began* after it ended in 2005. Had I died when I was 32, I never would have lived a day.

Still, on the topic of suicide, I can't draw a conclusion that sits right with me. Yes, I'm glad I was able to save my dad, and yes, I'm happy I got to share that last writing moment with him. But did that help *him,* or just me? Nothing ended the pain in his life until his life ended. I guess I think you should always have the right to choose when your life will end, and all the laws against that, all the medical establishment opposing it, and all the loved ones who refuse to accept it, are ultimately enfeebling, and deny the dignity of the human being. That said, I'm glad I never killed myself, and I hope nobody who reads this will ever kill themselves. Because if I had, you'd never have read these words. It can be a hard decision to live, but it's the only decision that allows other decisions, better choices and better possibilities for the future. There can always be a new story, a better story than the one we're living now, that we may feel stuck in now, but only if we let the story keep going.

18

Choosing to be

Ruth Kilner

It may seem unoriginal to begin this reflection with the most popular quote from all of English literature, but I could think of no better summary of my daily dialogue with suicide:

> *To be or not to be, that is the question.*
> (Hamlet, Act 3, Sc. 1, 57)

That is the question which, for as long as I can remember, I have asked myself each and every day. Do I have any fight left in me to tolerate these overwhelming feelings of self-hatred and anger, or should I just put a stop to it altogether?

In a report written by a psychiatrist I saw several years ago, I was described as having *suicidal ideation.* This in short means that I think about suicide regularly, but obviously have not successfully carried it out; otherwise I would not be writing this.

I wear a sleeve of reminders of my battles with self-harm; a coping strategy that through dialectical behavioural therapy (DBT) I have stopped, by and large. Although in the most part my harming has not been done with suicidal intent, I have found that seeing myself bleed and being aware of the power I hold with the blade – that I could end this suffering more or less instantly – has led me to the realisation of being alive, and has taken me out of my thoughts and into the moment; suddenly fearing for my life and perceiving it as somehow precious. This process of scaring myself into dealing with my overwhelming emotions is something I like to call *gothic mindfulness.*

When I was at school, kids used to notice my scarred arm and amongst other choice nicknames I was branded *suicide girl. But* it's not suicide; it is the opposite. It reminds me that I am alive. It reminds me I have the choice to be here or not, and that in itself is liberating. It's like skydiving, or any adrenaline-based sport. In my hands is the absolute power to end this misery, and today I choose not to. I choose to persevere.

Having said that, I did make one serious suicide attempt through an overdose of my antidepressants at the age of 17. At that time I was caught up in feelings of guilt, a myriad of destructive relationships, lack of direction, hatred of myself and the world, and desperate hopelessness. A lot of health professionals whom I saw seemed to think this was just a stage I was going through and that I would grow out of it: a female version of Holden Caulfield (the main character in J.D. Salinger's *The Catcher in the Rye*) if you will. One report from a psychiatrist in that era read, 'Ruth was casually dressed in black clothes'. This amused me, as I suspected that they deduced my attention-seeking behaviours were part of an alternative lifestyle choice. Unfortunately, ten years later I have proved them wrong, and though those feelings have evolved and matured, I am much the same.

I can't remember which SSRI I was on at the time, but after getting home from a distressing shift at work and craving the luxurious feeling of not having to wake up in the morning ever again, I washed down the whole pack and some painkillers with a bottle of wine. The rest of the sequence is blurry, but I recall later being in a room at the hospital and having to answer a psychologist's questions about why I had done it. Despite feeling groggy, I was fully present and aware of my surroundings. I knew that if I told him that I had in fact desperately wanted to die and I was disappointed that it hadn't worked, I would be sectioned and forced to stay in the hospital. I just wanted to get home to sleep off the hangover that was creeping in from the cocktail of drugs.

There are two ways of looking at my mental illness; I am either very lucky or perhaps unlucky to be rational, articulate and able to outsmart the psychologist. If I had been within a psychotic episode when I took the overdose, I would have ended up on a ward until professionals felt I was no longer a risk to myself. The truth is that I am constantly a controlled risk to myself. I knew what I needed to say in order to be released home, and through my best amateur dramatics performance, was deemed fit enough by someone who should have known better.

I have since read lots of horror stories about people taking overdoses ending up paralysed or with brain damage. This is not a technique I would try again, and to the horror of my therapist I recently declared that if I was going to do it again, I would do it properly. During a bleak depressive period in 2010, I planned routes to nearby high buildings I could jump from and sourced local suppliers where I could buy rope. I could buy a bottle of household chemical, drink it and do myself irreparable damage if I were found in time, and go through horrendous pain in the process.

Funding is tight and hospital beds scarce and I don't blame the hospital for letting me go that day. But it took another seven years for me to get the help I needed, and for that I had to pay privately and deal with psychiatrists who at times thought I seemed fine because I appeared middle class, well-spoken, and in control. Without meaning to be disrespectful or undermining towards people with illnesses who do lose touch with reality, I sometimes wish that I wasn't so aware of everything going on. The cacophony of critical, taunting voices in my mind is at times too much to handle. A useful tool I learnt in my DBT to deal with this is called 'passengers on the bus'. I pretend I am the bus driver and the intrusive thoughts are rowdy passengers. I acknowledge they are present, but ignore them and just get on with driving the bus. This sounds quite ridiculous, but it works for me.

I am aware that I am a high-functioning service user. Although I have been on Incapacity Benefit in the past, I have held down a job for the past two years, have studied to master's level and am now embarking on a PhD. I do not patronise or consider myself superior to others who are unable to live a seemingly functional life.

Suicide for me is a preventative cure. The daily choice I make to be here, living my life, is liberating and empowering. The knowledge that I exist voluntarily and that if things get just that bit worse or too overwhelming I can opt out makes the day-to-day symptoms I endure much more manageable. This self-bargaining has been going on for about 15 years. When I am finding things particularly difficult, I will say 'we'll give it a week' or 'see how you feel in two weeks'. I use this system to get through lots of things. If I think of my life as a whole, or sometimes even just a whole week, it becomes overwhelming.

Having borderline personality disorder (BPD) comes with its own unique challenges. It is widely misunderstood and perceived as a made-up, American disease for histrionic, hysterical, unbearable women. Whilst I don't deny being all of the above, I wouldn't say they were intrinsic character traits; more like unwanted symptoms. A turning point for BPD sufferers globally came in 2011 when American NFL player Brandon Marshall publicly admitted to suffering from the illness. A film is being made about his life entitled *Borderline Beast*. This public declaration can be likened to when British rugby player Gareth Thomas came out as being homosexual. Marshall is helping to highlight that anyone, even a butch sportsman, can be afflicted with this condition. I find it useful to share this example with people who are judgemental of my diagnosis.

Throughout my young life I have had many people, including close friends and family, advising me to 'snap out of it', 'think positive' and 'keep my chin up.' During a cognitive behavioural therapy session – an intervention that I found actually worsened my condition as I was forced to focus on negative thoughts rather than accept and diffuse them – the therapist enquired as to whether I had tried 'not thinking that everyone hates me'. The confusion amongst people who have enviably not experienced mental illness is that a thought process or feeling is done out of choice. Just as I could not choose to grow another arm if I had only one, I cannot click my fingers and change my mind. But I have learned to manage and cope with it better.

There are lots of reasons why I may be and feel the way I am. Traumatic things I have been through, perhaps a genetic predisposition, but analysing these possibilities can sink me further into the abyss. I am stuck with it, and my coping strategy is that I either make the best of it, or I opt out.

One of the main things that puts me off ending it all is what happens on the other side. Having been brought up Catholic – although I don't practise now – I was taught that suicide is a mortal sin. The gothic images of a burning inferno, howling souls in purgatory and sitting at the right hand of Lucifer himself for all eternity make the mundane reality of depression and intrusive thoughts seem strangely appealing and manageable.

The best way I can describe BPD is that you feel everything through a magnifying glass. Every tiny daily rejection, lack of reply, snide remark or criticism is blown up to gargantuan scale and is devastating. A positive spin-off is that it has made me very compassionate and empathetic, but through a constant desire for approval I have often people-pleased at my own expense. I crucify myself with guilt about friends and people in my life I have lost as I have abandoned them at times when I have been unwell, and they have been either scared or disbelieving when I've explained my absences. I have felt suicidal when rejected by such people.

It may seem horribly morbid to feel inspired and invigorated by the possibility of suicide. But for me, the trials and tribulations of my day-to-day existence are manageable if I constantly remind myself that there is a way out and that I am here out of choice.

Each day is a new and unwelcome battle, but I hope never to lose my fighting spirit again.

Learning/discussion points:

- People with personality disorders should be taken seriously when they present at a hospital or GP (general practitioner) practice with distressing symptoms; these experiences are very real and unpleasant and are not attention-seeking behaviours.

- Specialist help for BPD (borderline personality disorder), such as dialectical behaviour therapy, should be made available in all localities.

- Symptoms such as depression and anxiety should be investigated when they recur over an extended period of time, as they could be indicative of something more serious.

- People with mental illness may be defiant and declare that they are well, no longer need their medication, and stop taking it abruptly. GP practices should contact patients as part of an after-care procedure when it's noticed that their repeat prescription has ceased. Stopping medication 'cold-turkey' can lead to worsening of symptoms.

19

The ultimate barrier – for all those who never made it back

Tessa Glaze

After suffering a nervous breakdown in childhood it left the inevitable scars of anxiety that would dominate most aspects of my waking life. It manifested itself as social phobia and body dysmorphia and the underlying depression stole away any ability to concentrate and continue to learn.

In the early years my survival strategy was to avoid any situation where the inevitable panic attacks would catapult me into a world of all-consuming fear. It was at this time there became an awareness of a fog-like sensation that had taken up residency in my head, and every day became like wading through glue. Only years later did I recognise that this was the depression in its physical form. I developed a kind of dysfunctional coping strategy but at the same time my self-esteem went into free fall.

On reflection even then I would absorb negativity from others around me like a sponge. Throughout my teenage years going out in daylight became problematic except for attending school. My parents who were recently divorced were deeply concerned but medical intervention into childhood depression was still basically crude and relied on Valium which only served to tranquilise me.

Being so vulnerable I began to internalise comments made by others around me which only served to feed the body dysmorphia, and cause my self-esteem to plummet even further. The first time I experienced social phobia was during assembly at secondary school. We were seated in what seemed like hundreds of rows when the thought came to me that there was no escape. My whole body became racked by tremors that were alien to me. I slowly rose from my chair and walked the endless path along the centre of the assembly hall. From that day onwards my life would be controlled and dictated by fear, which would serve to wreak havoc with every aspect of my life.

The panic attacks were insidious and began to spread like the roots of a tree, throughout every activity at school and then during my home life. This caused me to isolate myself from people and become even more reclusive. This in turn evolved into a self-fulfilling prophecy whereby my fear of rejection was forever paramount and would become a foundation for all future relationships.

A more sinister strategy developed where I took on blame and guilt for issues that were not mine; this imploded after moving away from my original family to live with my mother and stepfather. After moving away to live at my mother's, on the surface it appeared that the transition went well, largely due to the arrival of a basset hound puppy called Sammy who became my constant companion. We had such a unique bond; she had been taken from her original family to a strange place – maybe because of this we shared a common ground. If things got too much I could always bury myself in her fur and she would comfort me, as we held on to each other for much-needed security as our world kept changing.

Sadly this relationship would not last when a decision was made to have her bred and we would then become separated. The desperation felt at the loss of my dog spiralled into guilt as I processed it as being my fault. It became impossible to forgive myself for not protesting more and ultimately allowing it to happen. The crushing guilt felt was all encompassing and the panic attacks would implode my school life and hold me a prisoner of my own anxiety.

When Sammy eventually died was the first time that suicidal thoughts entered my head. It's my belief that it was only childhood naivety that prevented me from putting a plan into place.

Respite eventually came with my first teenage romance, and my obsessive nature caused me to focus on this relationship and the problems subsided to an extent. But the anxiety was always just under the surface waiting to devour me given the right environment or circumstances.

It was during my early teenage years when feelings of self-consciousness turned into something more sinister, after beginning to apply heavy make-up every day – what wasn't realised was that a mask was actually being created. A shopping trip to London ended disastrously when my mother and sister refused to walk with me due to my appearance.

Although as an adult this incident can be perceived differently, my mind took on a new mantra. I wanted to run away from them, slip into the London streets and disappear forever. This would be the answer – to purge my family from the physical abomination I had become, once and for all.

This was probably the second time thoughts of suicide crept into my mind, but instead I continued to trail behind. How could I have possibly known then that more seeds were cultivating in my head, and the body dysmorphia would get steadily worse, because every time a destructive message was received in this way all past wounds would open up and begin to mentally bleed and fester. Words spoken by others can be perceived as a weapon that will continue to hurt and permeate.

Most of my teenage years would be spent closeted at home; if I did venture outside it would be totally dominated with an overwhelming desire to get back, to safety and obscurity. If there was dysfunction present in my relationships, I never really questioned it. My mother would always say she could not understand how I allowed everything to just happen to me.

The ability to protect myself appeared no longer to exist. When in the grips of a depressive illness, you become dehumanised to an extent. My parents were always deeply concerned about my problems, but even they could not possibly know how serious they had become.

After giving birth to my first daughter it was inevitable I guess that the depression would be compounded further as my own childhood issues rose to the surface. Struggling to cope we muddled through until after my second child was born. Then followed a period where I didn't appear to cope with my two small children, and feelings of dread were always present. I told my GP how desperate the feelings of depression were; he dismissed my cry for help and his reply was, 'You say you're depressed, well don't we all feel like that?' He would take his own life just a few years later.

Ironically although there was an awareness that something was dreadfully wrong, the depression became so entrenched it was part of me. Like an endless shadow taking away my ability to function on so many levels.

My marriage ended when my youngest child was three years old, and I found my husband with another woman in our home. It was Christmas and although a shock it also felt so predictable, and again his betrayal caused only to feed my fear of desertion. This also caused me to become extremely vulnerable regarding being taken advantage of; it always seemed to be the case and my hopeless naivety and lack of self-esteem would appear to collude with this.

My next relationship, with Michael, lasted almost seven years and again was obsessive because I was so frightened of loss and abandonment. My partner Michael died suddenly and another mental breakdown occurred. The shock of losing him was so overwhelming the bereavement became like a kind of madness in itself.

The horrendous situation was made even worse as Michael's family opposed provision being made for me and my children; in spite of the fact that I was helping him with his business and financially dependent on him at the time of his death. If I had been mentally strong enough I would have persevered with the legal claim, but I crumbled under the pressure. My mother was so concerned about my state of mind she warned me that if things didn't improve she feared I would get dangerously ill.

A life choice I made some time later would prove to rear all my mental health problems to a head, and another breakdown occurred whereby I hardly left my home at all for five years.

In spite of all the problems there always appeared to be present an inner strength that provided me with a spirit to survive.

Years later my mother contracted dementia. She had always been a driving force and constant source of love and inspiration throughout the years living with this invisible illness. I was a main carer for Mum for ten years and at times I would question who was guiding who. The insidious lows would make it almost impossible to help her when she needed me the most, but I tried so ridiculously hard to keep it all going. This would be the beginning of a series of more serious mental breakdowns.

Towards the end of her life I began to experience a preoccupation with my own death and a desire to construct a suicide plan. All the problems for almost 40 years had built to a crisis point and the thoughts became all consuming. Losing my mother and the onset of my own ageing process was causing life to be impossible and I began to be plagued by morbid thoughts.

'How could I live in a world full of people and not be seen?' I would ponder constantly as destructive thoughts ravaged through my tormented mind. Social phobia had been my lonely companion for so long. Hovering above me like an albatross with no intention of releasing me from its grip.

Any desire to survive was lost to me almost as if everything was being stripped away until this was the only choice left. There was a vague awareness that I was seeking refuge for a final resting place in a burial home.

A strange acceptance developed of what my intentions were as my mind continued to shut down to alternatives, reacting in the same way as organs during a terminal illness. My twisted logic was that the only way to achieve being totally hidden was to be buried deeply underground, and it was not possible to achieve this while still alive; hidden at home, always fearing venturing outside and the risk of being seen. I had lived such a huge part of my life this way and the demons in my head were causing me to give up the fight. Any optimism or hope was lost to me and my spirit was ultimately broken.

My family were obviously horrified by my perception; it was particularly distressing for my daughters who struggled to understand. I tried to explain how my reflection was perceived as something which only served to frighten and disgust me. No one could possibly realise that the illness was running riot, wreaking havoc and using the body dysmorphia as its weapon of destruction. There is a very high suicide rate amongst sufferers of body dysmorphia, possibly because there really is no other ultimate escape from your own self.

The mental fog became ever more stagnant; at one point the ability to write my own name became alien to me, as if all sense of self had begun to disappear. This was the point where my suicide began to be planned because all the escape hatches appeared to be closing. Planning and orchestrating my own death became all consuming, a twisted dysfunctional driving force. I reasoned that the only escape from the darkness my life had become was to transcend further into just that.

There was an occasion where on returning to my car at the top of a multistorey car park, I just wanted to jump and end it all. It seemed the only obstacle in my way were the shoppers returning to their own cars.

When my partner Steve said he was planning a fishing trip I grabbed this as an opportunity to put my own plan in place. The last thing to remain is the spirit and mine was abandoning me as I climbed the stairs and gazed long and hard at the banister. Looking down I realised that I could tie a rope and hang there until Steve returned and found me. I don't remember being aware that in effect I was constructing my own gallows. The hanging process did not faze me at all but suddenly the realisation of what Steve would encounter registered and stopped me in my tracks. I had a mental vision of him coming home and having to cut me down. I realised that it simply wasn't feasible to put him through this. The truth was that Steve would then be haunted by this memory and it became obvious I could not carry this out. The girls and grandchildren and my mother and father were there in the equation and this was the only defining factor. Like an invisible lifeline had be thrown which caused me to abandon the rope, while all the time my mind was scanning for another option.

Everything evolves from childhood and one of my happiest memories has always been visiting Dreamland and riding on the ghost train. The sheer excitement mixed with fear as we rode through the crudely constructed cobwebs has stayed with me. Maybe that was the reason for my ultimate choice of ending my life by train. It would also be quick and have the added bonus of almost eradicating my tired mind and body in an instant. Even being told once by a hospital worker that the physical remains of someone who chooses death by train arrive at the mortuary via the back door did not influence me to change my mind.

Death was so close I could almost touch it and my waking thoughts became consumed with desperation for endless sleep. To never again be stricken with fear and self-loathing was a delicious concept and suicide became my ultimate coping strategy. A new mindset evolved which would serve to cultivate death as something to be desired not feared. If only the long sleep could be achieved there would no more suffering, or having to live like a computer with a virus.

A strange phenomenon began to take root in the form of total loss of interest or motivation.

My only focus appeared to be how I was going to commit this final act, and visualising my funeral service, nothing could be voiced, as everything I had to put in place had to be done meticulously but without raising suspicion.

Any logic or desire to survive was evaporating as I appeared to transcend through layers of despair with a grim determination to become ultimately invisible. I became aware of a sensation and appeared to be gravitating away from everyone that I loved; almost as if I was to remain static, the act could not be carried out.

Intricate Catholic influences from childhood where we were told of the soul being sent to purgatory appeared to have no effect, because my existence itself had become a living hell.

During this preoccupation a local man took his life in this way at the nearby railway station. The phone rang and my youngest daughter spoke in frantic tones, 'Mum, I just heard about the body on the line … Mum, I thought it was you.'

These words changed everything and in a single moment the simple truth was staring me in the face. I had almost got to the level which was to go beyond the planning but remain convinced this is the defining factor whereby everything and everyone would become lost. I therefore conclude that it is not a decision that is left available to the ones who succeed in taking their own life. During the stripping-down process if the bonds are taken away from us surely this is no longer a matter of choice.

This experience has left me with no doubt that had I progressed beyond this stage it would have been the point of no return. To this day I recognise that my continued existence is due to surviving a near-death experience. You have to go that deep into the abyss to realise it is only one step from oblivion, and as the instinct to survive returned I gained the strength to contact my GP. His words were for me to be treated as an emergency, which enabled me to receive medical intervention that ultimately saved my life.

An insight into the depths the mind can go to has left me with a conviction that suicide victims are ultimately left with no alternative. Therefore I strongly oppose the opinion that it is a selfish act, and it has left me without any doubt this occurs when ultimately the chains that bind us to loved ones serve to cut loose.

I was extremely fortunate to have a mental health specialist who provided me with medication and therapy to set me on the path to recovery. In recovery all emotions buried for so long began to return, alongside my ability to write which had become lost for so long in the illness.

Sadly the relationship with my sisters has never recovered from being split as children. They managed to maintain their bond but it never seemed possible to regain what we once had all those years ago.

The only connection I have now with trains is the sound of them rumbling in the distance; I hear them as they journey back and forth from London. Along this route they pass by where my beloved mother is buried. It may seem obscure but it brings her close to me.

Every day the realisation is with me that I could so easily have ended my life and ultimately missed so much. These days my family and grandchildren are a constant source of delight and it is abhorrent to me to realise that I could have so easily not made it back. If my reflection is seen in their eyes it is seen for what it is, and is no longer something to fear.

Learning/discussion points:

- I have experienced at times that mental health professionals over-scrutinise my appearance and behaviour for confirmation of my current mental state. I have found this to be demeaning and also stigmatising.

- I believe it would be beneficial if we were provided with more information regarding the long-term use of antidepressant medication. I experience an improvement in my mental health on the medication, but still experience devastating low episodes and the subsequent feelings of suicide.

20

Semi-suicidal

Helen Harrop

I am standing by the sink in our kitchen. I am holding a knife in my right hand. I am pressing the very tip of the blade hard against the vein that runs up my left wrist. I want to puncture the vein and let some blood flow but my skin is unyielding and resists my efforts. I am not trying to kill myself but a part of me wants to know how easy it will be to slit open that vein if I do decide to die. I'm disheartened to discover that it will be much harder than I have imagined.

Arguably this is the closest I have come to acting on my suicidal impulses. Looking back I can see that it represents the summit of a mountain that I have been desperately trying not to climb and yet somehow I find myself standing here pressing a knife into my wrist. I shrug off my death wish once more and carry on unloading our dishwasher.

At that moment it was less than six months since my GP had diagnosed me with severe chronic depression and prescribed the minimum daily dose of citalopram. I was now up to the maximum dosage of 30 mg and the safety net that I had hoped antidepressants would provide has failed to materialise. In one of our weekly sessions I tell my therapist that I feel as though I wake up every morning looking into the abyss and have to spend the rest of the day inching my way back from the cliff's edge. And then I go to bed, eventually fall asleep and wake up the next morning to find myself at the cliff's edge once more.

I'd been battling with this death wish for much of my adult life but by this point it had evolved from an occasional intrusive brutal thought, often involving being instantly wiped out by a passing lorry, to thoughts that were becoming more frequent, more deliberate and more insistent. And there was a

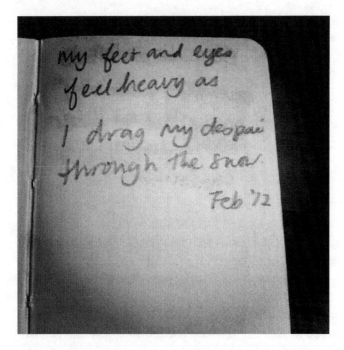

voice that had started accompanying the thoughts. The voice had started repeatedly whispering 'Do It!' as a train pulled into the platform or as a bus hurtled by at the traffic lights. So far another voice inside me had always dismissed the whisper but that voice seemed to be fading fast and the whispering voice was getting louder. I am terrified that the whispering voice will win out, deeply ashamed that I seem to be failing at the simple task of being human and exhausted by my seemingly Sisyphean struggle. More than anything I just want the battle to be over – one way or the other.

In truth I wasn't scared of dying but I was scared of the legacy my suicide would leave behind for the people I knew. Particularly those I loved. My husband. My twin sister. My mum. My grandma. My older sister and her young children (who are still struggling to cope with the unexpected death of my brother-in-law). My aunts, uncles and my cousins. My best friend. My work colleagues. My therapist. My wider circle of friends. My next-door neighbours. Even the 2000 people who followed me on Twitter. I worried that one day I would stop worrying about what my death would do to them. Because when that day arrived I would be free to jump. In a notebook I wrote: 'too scared to live, too brave to die'. But I didn't feel brave – I felt pathetic and I felt trapped by my own cowardice. I wanted to not exist, to stop breathing, to fade away – I did not want to take my own life. I couldn't bring myself to commit suicide but by this point it was the only solution that held any hope. I wanted my death to be painless, painless for me and painless for those I would be leaving behind. My fear of a failed attempt and of the suffering a successful attempt would cause for those who know me was one of the only things keeping me alive. One day I was hit by the realisation that the only way I could kill myself without hurting anyone else would be to take the entire planet out with me – the thought is absurd, brutal, deeply shocking and was the first glimpse I got of the deeply buried anger that lay beneath my depression and my tendency towards self-destruction.

At the time I had no idea of how close to the edge I was in reality and whether I would ever act on my suicidal impulses, but I stepped up the precautionary measures I'd been taking for years. While I'm waiting at tube stations in London I force myself to stand with my back pressed against the back wall away from the platform edge until the arriving train has come to a halt. When my husband hands me a large box of 400 mg ibuprofen I take one strip from the box and ask him to store the rest at work. And as the deathly whispering got louder I devised delaying tactics and made bargains with myself to buy extra time – I started knitting a blanket 400 stitches wide and internally agreed not to kill myself before the blanket was finished.

I clung onto lines from songs, poems and books as if they were life rafts, all the while staying almost silent about my battle to everyone except my GP, my therapist, my husband, my twin sister. Everyone I met on a day-to-day basis would scarcely have suspected I had depression let alone guess that I was suicidal – it is no wonder that depression is sometimes called 'the grinning madness'. I lived in fear of anyone uttering the phrase 'Are you "okay"?' with anything close to genuine concern – I was convinced that I would completely fall apart. The silence is cast iron, completely self-imposed, and I didn't consider breaking it for even a moment.

I'm walking across Ouse Bridge on my way home from work. I stop halfway across to stare into the barely moving, thick inky water below. I feel the weight of the laptop and other belongings in the rucksack I'm carrying on my back. I'm certain that if I walk back over the bridge and make my way to the river's edge then I can slip into that inviting darkness and disappear with barely a ripple; the weight of my rucksack enough to drag me down to the river bed.

The impulse is echoed in the opening lines from an unfinished poem I'd scrawled on the back of an envelope a few months beforehand:

> *Let's fill our pockets*
> *With the rocks we find*
> *And take our tears*
> *Back to the sea;*
>
> *We'll walk into the river,*
> *We'll walk into the stream,*
> *We'll walk to the bottom*
> *Of the wave-ridden lake;*
>
> *We'll wait in the depths*
> *With our faith, hope and dreams;*
> *Until the bubbles stop rising,*
> *Until the air leaves our lungs,*
> *Until we breathe our last breath,*
> *Until our desolation drowns.*

My thoughts are jolted back to reality; someone might see me going under. That someone might jump in to save me. And that someone might lose their life trying to save mine. I shrug the thoughts away and carry on home but as I walk away I launch an internal investigation to try and establish what this morbid part of me thinks it will gain from sinking below the surface of the Ouse. I ask myself what I was feeling as I looked down into the dark river and the response that comes back is immediate: a feeling of comfort, a sense of sanctuary. Shortly after that night I make contact with the Maytree Respite Centre in London, a sanctuary for the suicidal.

As I make my way across London to the Maytree Centre, on an unseasonably warm and sunny morning in April 2012, I make one last bargain with myself – I won't kill myself until after my stay at the Maytree. As my anxiety levels rise on the train, I put my headphones in my ears and cocoon myself in The Silent League's songs to keep me safe during my journey. I arrive at their front door with a feeling that could best be described as chronic battle fatigue and I surrender myself completely to their care for five days. While I'm there I sleep, talk, eat, knit, read, laugh and cry. In my cosy attic bedroom, in the sun-filled garden, at the dinner table and in the one-to-one therapy sessions I finally find the sanctuary I've been so desperately searching for. In one of the individual therapy sessions one of the directors tells me that she has a picture of me in her mind – I'm standing on the hellishly hot banks of a river and cannot bring myself to jump into the cool, revitalising waters of the stream that is running alongside me, even though I know how much better I will feel once I do. I worry that I will leave after four nights and will still be afflicted by the feeling of paralysis that has plagued me for so many years. On the sheet of paper left by my bedside table I write, 'I have a river of tears trapped inside me' – I feel like I have both a volcano about to erupt and a dam about to burst inside me. A day later I scribble the words 'I am already dead inside' and part of me realises that killing myself would be utterly pointless because something in me has already been murdered many, many years earlier. The thought is much more comforting than it probably sounds.

In one of my last one-to-one sessions the same director tells me she hopes that even though I can't yet take off my armour she hoped that my time at the Maytree had at least thinned it out a little. As I prepare to leave the next day I feel like a different person. In fact I feel like a person, full stop – I have a fledgling sense of self for the first time in living memory. And as my train back to York pulls out of King's Cross Station I have a sense of 'going home' for the first time too. I look out of the window and see a small stream glinting alongside the train tracks and I write in my notebook: 'a river of kindness is following me home'.

I still don't understand exactly how or why but my persistent suicidal thoughts disappeared overnight, as if a switch in my head had been flipped to 'off' while I was sleeping. But I do know that I no longer see bridges, rivers, roads, train lines, knives and painkillers as weapons that I can use to kill myself. The void that I woke up next to every morning has also receded from view and the grinding, aching, empty nothingness that I once felt is already hard for me to imagine. And I suddenly feel like I've not only discarded my battle-worn armour, I've removed myself from the battlefield completely.

When I look back at what I went through it is my self-imposed vow of silence that I still find chilling, and I worry that if the darkness envelopes me again in the future I would stay silent once more. So I feel like I have a moral duty to break my own silence about what I went through while I can and also speak up about my experiences on behalf of those people who cannot yet bring themselves to reach out and let someone know that they are drowning inside. My weekly therapy sessions continue, possibly to be succeeded by group therapy sessions in the near future. I still have a lot of work to do around safeguarding myself and building a resilient sense of self but I no longer feel like I'm doing so on borrowed time – I now have my whole lifetime to unravel and embrace the mystery that makes me who I am.

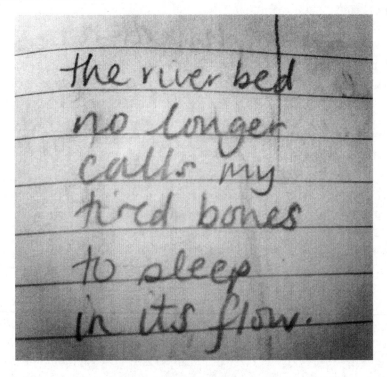

the river bed
no longer
calls my
tired bones
to sleep
in its flow.

Learning/discussion points:

- At the height of my suicidal crisis I was desperately searching for two things: respite from my dark thoughts and hope that I would recover. Frontline mental health and GP services should pay attention to how their interactions provide, or deny, respite and hope to suicidal people.

- I still don't have a personal safety plan in place that I can follow when my mood drops, and this leaves me vulnerable if my suicidal thoughts ever return. It would be good to receive post-crisis support to help me build a safety net while I'm coping well, which will then be there to catch me in the early stages of any mental health crisis.

- When I try to encourage the people I know to reach out to those around them who might be distressed, the overwhelming response is that people aren't sure what they should say and are worried they might make matters worse by saying the wrong thing. If everyone who worked in a public-facing role was trained in mental-health first aid and taught listening skills that they could use at home as well as at work, our society would quickly become one where it is OK to talk about our mental health struggles.

- If my GP or therapist had handed me a pamphlet that explains depression and suicide to family, friends and colleagues, that would have helped a great deal and assisted me in becoming my own advocate at home and work.

Untitled

21

Naomi

Having suffered with depression for years, I am no stranger to suicidal feelings. I have even attempted it in the past, and I've been collecting tablets for years. It always felt like an option; not only that, but I also felt as though it was inevitable that my life would end that way.

In October 2011, my friend's dad committed suicide. She found him. My wonderful, amazing, beautiful friend got home from school one day to find her dad, no longer alive. When I found out, I could barely function. I rang my counsellor and somehow made it to the clinic where I sat in shock until my parents could collect me. This man, this talented man who was always smiling and meant so much to so many people, had taken his own life. And my 17-year-old friend and her 14-year-old brother had found him.

I had known he'd been struggling. My friend had mentioned it to me a week or so before. He had started new antidepressants and they were having negative side effects on him. Her parents hadn't been sharing a bed. But I never dreamt it would end like this.

The next day, I visited my friend. She was white as a sheet, clutching her teddy. Her eyes were filled with horror. She kept getting flashbacks about what had happened. She kept repeating the same things over and over. Her mum was a mess. She'd aged about 20 years overnight. I sat with my friend, we talked a bit, but there wasn't much to say. We hugged a lot.

I went to his funeral. Hundreds of people were there. He was an integral part of the community. People were saying how they'd seen him only days before and everything seemed fine. He had never mentioned that things were so bad. He was a good man: had you not known, you would never have suspected that depression lay within him. He took part in many community events and was never without a smile. He left behind two beautiful young children and a loving wife, as well as other friends and family.

Having seen this event, suicide is no longer an option for me. I still struggle, I still get suicidal thoughts, but I will never forget my friend's face the day I saw her after it had happened. Whatever is going on in my life, I have to live; there is no choice any more.

SURVIVING SUICIDE

22

Suicide – my story

Anonymous

For those people who travel regularly on the Underground in London, the sight of a white board with a handwritten message announcing delays due to 'passenger action' or a 'person being on the line' is a familiar sight. For commuters, this is an added annoyance, another hindrance to getting to work or home. I feel something different when I see those signs. They make my stomach flip. I can't help wondering what has led that person to feel so desperate that they felt they had no other choice but to step off the edge of the platform in front of a train.

Why do I feel like that? Because I have been that person; I felt I had no other choice. I felt I was not worthy to live. I felt I was of no value to my friends, my family, my partner and, worst of all, I felt I was of no value to my 10-year-old son and 20-month-old daughter. (In my right mind, my non-depressed brain, I know how wrong that is.) I could see no future. Most importantly, I had no hope. I could not bear to exist one moment more with the torture of the depressive thoughts that had overtaken me, not for the first time in my life. (To anyone who has not experienced depression, 'torture' might appear to be a strong word, but for me it is the only word that comes close to the relentless, exhausting whirl of negativity and self-criticism that overtakes me and which I become incapable of stopping. 'Turmoil' understates this process.) So that, I suppose in short, is what drove me to step off the edge of the platform, in front of a tube train pulling into the station, one sunny Monday morning in July, when it should have just been another day at work.

I had left my daughter with the child minder. She happily toddled off to play after I had hugged and kissed her goodbye, outwardly normal. Inwardly, I thought it was the last goodbye.

My son was in the car with my partner when he dropped me off at the tube station. I waved them goodbye. After the event, my partner said that he had noticed I was quiet on the journey, a little withdrawn, and that when he got back home a couple of hours later, in a sense he was not surprised to be greeted by two transport policemen waiting on the doorstep. Approaching home, he had heard reports on the radio of delays on the tube.

Looking back I cannot imagine how I managed to get through that morning's routine activities of getting myself and the kids ready, whilst knowing that I had made a decision to do what I did when I got to the station. I can actually picture myself walking down the steps on to the platform. I can see the clothes that I was wearing (and which later, in their blood-stained state, were returned to me when I was in hospital). These images are vivid but memories of how I actually felt are not so clear. I was fearful but knew that I was going to carry out what had run around my head during two nights of very little sleep. I remember thinking that I had to do something that would work, that would finish me off.

What was the build-up to this? A noticeable weight loss and steadily increasing sleeplessness were all too familiar symptoms. I tried to ignore the blanket of depression enveloping me as it had done on other occasions. At a routine doctor's appointment at my mental health centre only days before (I had been attending there since an episode of post-natal depression following my daughter's birth), I met with yet another locum doctor who of course could make no comparison of my mental state to my previous visit as she had never met me before. Nor had she the time probably to read my notes in which it was documented that I could 'decline rapidly'. In our short time together I told her about my sister's death, three months earlier, my decision to take a redundancy and my planned trip overseas with my kids. However I am sure I was convincing in my claims that I was coping. I believe her recommendations were to try and relax and let myself enjoy my trip.

Over the following days, what happened was what the notes predicted. I declined rapidly. The feelings of negativity and futility intensified. I felt entirely without hope. Without hope for a future. Without hope that I would be able to cope with the ever-increasing feelings of worthlessness and failure that were filling my head at all times.

Although I had had previous episodes of depression and come out of them, thanks to a combination of drugs and talking therapies, at that time I could not believe in any hope of recovery and what's more I did not believe that I deserved to recover.

I considered myself to be worthless. Why could I not 'get through' things like everyone else? I mentally gave myself no sympathy for having recently lost a sister to breast cancer. At that time, I was the failure. The one who could not cope like everyone else.

For me, comparing myself to others has always been a recurring theme. Judging myself to be not as good, not as worthwhile, not as emotionally strong, is the particular stick that I choose to beat myself with. As a result, what I most want for my children is that they have a strong sense of self-worth.

Looking back now I can see that I was emotionally exhausted at that time. I was grieving as well. The thought of fighting off the depression seemed impossible. When I am in a depression, it is hard, almost impossible, to imagine feeling any other way. But on that particular occasion, all these emotions were more intense. It was different. I felt so desperate. I felt there was no way out, other than to end everything, to end my life; that was the only option.

It was not the first time I had 'attempted suicide'. I had taken drug overdoses. The first, when I was 19 and at college. With hindsight, I can see that it was not an attempt to commit suicide. It genuinely was – to use a cliché – 'a cry for help'. I was suffering. My first serious relationship had come to an end. I was feeling rejected, lonely, worthless and incapable of telling anyone how bad I felt. I clearly remember my best friend being so angry 'that I did not tell her how bad I felt'. To tell the truth, I am not sure if I did try to tell her and she did not listen, or whether, as I have on many other occasions, kept my emotions locked up inside. It was a rather dramatic gesture.

I would probably be defined by most people I know as outgoing, at times the life and soul of the party, and they would be surprised that I ever have difficulty showing how I feel. Showing how people want me to feel comes easy; I like to please. But being totally honest about how I really feel is a struggle – which has made embracing talking therapies rather difficult.

There were a couple of other occasions which, with the knowledge I have now about myself and about how depression affects me (acquired through numerous depressive episodes, therapy of varying quality, much reading and self-teaching), were also cries for help. It is almost as if at times, I feel I am going to explode with negativity and self-criticism. I become incapable of containing the emotions, getting through another day with the thoughts in my head – the torture. And that I cannot convey how bad I feel and therefore an action speaks louder than the words I cannot seem to speak.

But making other people realise how bad I was feeling was not my intention when I went to the Tube station that morning. My decision and action that day was to end my life. I did not feel I deserved to live. It was not like any other previous occasion and it is the one time that I believe I was truly suicidal.

I have been asked the question by mental health professionals, 'Did you leave a note?', and am never quite sure whether leaving a note is the indicator of whether a person is serious about their intention to take their life or not. I did not leave a note but I know that my intention that day was more serious than at any other time in my life.

What was it that brought me to the point of being suicidal? Truly suicidal. These things do not happen overnight. Most psychiatrists I have ever come into contact with very readily pinpoint the death of my father when I was 14 (or to be more precise, his disappearance – his body was never found) as being the key contributing factor that has defined my mental health as an adult. That event, it would seem, set me up as a likely candidate for depression – other explanations being a natural pre-disposition, perhaps a hormonal imbalance. Who knows? It seems no one, with total certainty. I wish I did know the absolute 'why' as it would possibly give me the absolute answer as to 'how' I could avoid it happening again.

I have had therapy, I have read books, I have talked to fellow sufferers. I take drugs (reluctantly at times) to keep the depression at bay. Can I prevent the return of suicidal feelings? I want to.

Just to finish my story. Whether I was hit by the train or fell to one side of it, I don't know for sure. The last thing I remember is a voice crying out behind me. I think it was a woman's. She must have realised what I was doing. I feel terrible to have submitted her to that experience. My back was broken in three places and I needed to have two vertebrae fused as a result. My neck was also broken and I was lucky not to have been paralysed. I needed to wear a halo traction for 12 weeks – a device that prevented me from moving my neck and head and gave the bones the opportunity to heal. This entailed having four screws screwed into my skull. I still have the marks on my forehead. I also have a large scar on my leg but apart from that you would never know what had happened to me.

The internal injuries have taken far longer to heal. To even be writing this story is such a huge step for me. For years I have felt so ashamed of what I tried to do and of the pain and suffering I could have caused my children.

From the moment I came round in intensive care, I knew that I wanted to be alive. The big focus was on my physical injuries and for several months I received no mental health support apart from antidepressants (which I had to request on the ward – they were not offered). Just writing this now, I realise how well I did all on my own. There were many hours of reflection whilst I was on the ward in the seven weeks I spent there. Plus the months later wearing a plaster that replaced my halo traction. Did the physical needs of my body override everything else? Possibly. I can't remember being filled with hope for the future. But similarly I know I was not without hope in the way that I was when I went into that Tube station that morning. My focus was on the physical hurdles of sheer survival. It was a year after that the mental repercussions of my action took hold. An episode of depression took grip and that was when I started to deal with what I had done. And I am still dealing with it to this day but to varying degrees. I have yet to tell my daughter what happened. I want her to hear the story from me and not from anyone else.

It is over ten years now since the event. My ability to recognise the symptoms of depression and, more importantly, acknowledge and deal with them have come a long way. Volunteering at a refuge for the suicidal, Maytree, has also helped me hugely as I believe that my experience can be turned into something positive by sharing my experience and my survival with others who are in that dark place of hopelessness.

And that ultimately would be how I would define feeling suicidal. It is feeling without hope.

23

The secrets of suicide

Dawn Willis

There are secrets in us all asking to be unbound and to be spoken of freely, without shame, allowing us to leave them in the past where they belong. They then become an experience and something we have gained wisdom from, no longer a burden to be borne alone.

This is just one of my secrets of suicide.

I never imagined I'd live beyond 19 years – I knew it in fact, I knew it from an early age. When I would try to imagine my grown-up self there was nothing to see, just a void, a kind of peaceful emptiness, and that was something I had no fear of and actually looked forward to. I suppose the child in me was trying to imagine what it would be like to be a 'grown up' and to be free from abuse, able to make my own choices, and my mind just couldn't see that picture, so I decided the 'void' seemed a particularly appealing destination.

As time went on, the urge to gain early entry to that void I was anticipating with such enthusiasm became quite overwhelming. There were a series of events, traumas in my childhood and then early teens, which had affected me with such magnitude that I felt like an observer, as if I was watching my own life as a harrowing documentary on a big screen, a story being played out by people I knew but had no under-standing of.

And it would be a scene from this drama in which I would decide at only 15 years old that it was time to leave the scary overwhelming world of my childhood and take a step into the calm depths of a welcoming death.

I had a boyfriend, and I was blossoming. Suddenly I'd gone from being the 'ugly' girl in school to a popular and sought-after young woman. It was bewildering – I had no experience of people liking me. It was as if when Spandau Ballet and Duran Duran brought flamboyance to the 1980s a lid was placed firmly on the bleakness of my early teenage years. It was overwhelming, but not unwelcome, and I was part of something, involved even – and I needed it to be normal, like it was for other kids. I wanted to be the same.

Suddenly I was allowed some make-up, and my mother began to allow me to choose some of my own clothes. I had friends, and boys paid me attention and I was excited and nervous. It felt like things were just going to be OK – at last, I was going to be like the other girls.

My boyfriend, such a sweet boy, younger than me but so much more mature, and safe – he was kind. He didn't want sex from me and I had no idea I was expected to have given it. He just liked being with me, talking to me, laughing, kissing. I suppose it was very old fashioned, sweet even, and that's why it felt so good.

I had to leave him to go on a family caravan holiday, but I promised to write every day. Maturing and voluptuous I was awkwardly aware of the effect of my sexuality, and my mother's orders that I wore bikinis and make the most of the British summer meant that I was very self-conscious. I also knew my period, or my 'doings' as my mother would almost shamefully refer to them, were due whilst on this holiday. I couldn't bear the 'Dr White's' sanitary belt and towels she insisted I wear because I was a child. I feared they'd show under my shorts, so I sneaked out of the caravan with my holiday savings, and bought 'tampons' – those secret little wrapped items all my friends were allowed to use. My mother demanded to know when my period arrived, so she could issue my sanitary protection, and I kept up a great presence of using the dreaded belt and towels, whilst secretly using the tampons. It felt good, I felt grown up and I felt happy.

I'd been to post a letter to my boyfriend – I can't remember what it said, but I imagine it was full of my teenage angst at being apart from him. She was waiting for me, my mother, at the caravan door. I knew I was in trouble by the set of her face and the tone of her eyes – her eyes always changed when she was angry. They'd sharpen, and the blue would become more intense. I think I remember even guessing what I was in trouble for.

Once I was inside she said, 'What have you been doing with the sanitary towels?'

'Putting them in the bin Mam, not down the toilet like you said.'

'So why are they clean then?' she asked, pointing to several she'd retrieved from the rubbish.

I cringed with humiliation, looking at the towels I'd carefully wrapped in toilet roll, laid out on the caravan table. 'It's not very heavy this time,' I said, meaning my flow.

'So why is the belt hidden under the carpet in the caravan bedroom then?' she asked. 'And whose are these?' she demanded, holding out my precious box of tampons.

'I don't know,' I said.

And that's when she hit me, and kept hitting me whilst shouting, 'You are nothing but a slut, these are for married women, not children. You are disgusting.'

Her tirade went on; she hit me so hard I bounced off the caravan walls. I imagined everyone on the site could hear every word she said. She berated me for having a boyfriend, and said she'd be putting a stop to that. She insinuated I'd had sex, and somehow when I look back that's all I can recall from that holiday.

I can't remember going home, or how she stopped me seeing my boyfriend, but it happened and I was, again, different. Alone and outside and wondering why I just couldn't seem to work out what I was meant to do to fit in. Everything had changed again.

Paracetamol, I don't know why. Perhaps I'd read it in a magazine. I took a lot, and I wandered the Haymarket in Newcastle upon Tyne waiting to fall down in the street and die. And I kept walking, amongst busy commuters, students and families, but still I didn't faint, still I didn't die. I felt sick and disorientated. I bought aspirin, took quite a number of these, and still I wasn't getting any closer to the void. I panicked.

I told Uncle Tony, and he was calm. He phoned the hospital and, at my terrified insistence, only my dad at that stage.

I don't recall much else – I know my dad was very sad, and my mother was angry and sad. I was referred to a psychiatrist, a wonderful man, who talked to me, and who told me my 'secrets' were safe with him, and I told him many.

Then one day he was taken from me. My mother had insisted on seeing him, on demanding to know what I talked about, and I can only assume he maintained my confidences because after five sessions she decided I'd see him no more, declaring him 'rubbish', and saying, 'Who does he think he is, saying it's about me? It's you, you are just attention seeking, and I'm not having it.'

I was trapped again, lost, and I began to wait, quietly and patiently, until the day I knew I would die, the day I could enter the Void.

Endnote

I didn't enter the Void at 19 – I made it beyond – and as the parent of three wonderful children I am pleased to say it was a blessing.

Suicide is not 'painless'. It would become apparent as I got older that I have a diagnosis of bipolar and post-traumatic stress disorder, and there have been times when the symptoms have been so unbearably difficult to cope with that I have tried desperately to take my own life.

Suicide is a selfish thought, yet not for the reasons you would imagine. It's not 'selfish' because it will hurt those you leave bereft. It's more about the need to be free from mental pain, which is as equally unbearable as physical. It's also about a powerful belief that those you love most will truly be better off without you. The guilt associated with the periods of mental ill health, which mean family members have to cope, care and adapt, is soul destroying, and a desire to 'free them' seems only natural and fair. Suicidal feelings, actions and thoughts are symptoms of an illness and should bear no shame for the sufferer, yet still society sees it as an act born of cowardice and selfishness.

Learning/discussion points:

- When I felt so desperate and so confused as a young woman, I couldn't imagine how I could ever get past the horror of it all, couldn't see how I would ever be anything other than a lonely scared child. Today I look back as a successful mature woman, the mother of three children and someone who has not only survived but has been strengthened by learning how to live with a diagnosis of bipolar disorder.

- People need not be afraid of mental illness affecting them. They need to concern themselves more with working at the discovery of their own recovery, to look at their aspirations and then figure out how they will achieve them despite their diagnosis.

- Diagnosis matters not; judge me by my diagnosis would you? That is my motto and it gives me strength.

24

The suicide note is not my story (*or* the suicide note does not play my song)

Dolly Sen

My first encounter with suicide was aged 14.

I didn't have a great childhood, in fact it was an extremely abusive one, but that wasn't the reason for my first attempt, not directly anyway.

I was 14 in 1984 and had a Sunday ritual of listening to the top 30 on the radio, with a tape deck at the ready to record any songs that took my fancy. Suddenly, a dark, demonic, gravel-choked voice boomed from the radio programme, saying, 'How much do you want?' It was a sentence I didn't understand and it scared me. I unplugged the radio, the music stopped, but the scary voice continued. 'I am the universe. I choose whether you live or breathe.'

That was the start of me hearing voices. What had brought me up to that point was a life of horror. I was born in London in 1970. My childhood was not a happy one: Physical, emotional, mental, sexual abuse, racism, poverty, neglect, bullying, and more, skinned me emotionally until I was only bone and pain. Most importantly there wasn't any hope. You don't need to search for the neurotransmitter that caused my psychosis when you can see the life I had to live before my mind finally collapsed.

Over the following week, the voices became more frequent and more harrowing: they were talking about raping me in my sleep. The visual hallucinations I had went from ghostly shadows on the Monday to full-blown demons on the Friday, threatening to kill my family if I didn't do as they dictated. When people tell me considering suicide is selfish, I wonder what they would do if they saw demons chasing them and threatening their families. The demons told me to kill myself, or my brothers and sisters would be tortured. That alone might have been reason enough to motivate my first attempt, but the overwhelming fear and terror of the experience choked my mind and throttled my heart, and just feeling totally and utterly unloved, pushed me over the edge.

Psychosis touches your heart, mind, and soul, and turns it all in on itself, like a knot that has no beginning or end. It turns your life into a ghost train ride without end. You are so haunted by spectres and on the edge of your seat with fear for what seems like forever. Imagine a nightmare so horrible you have to open your eyes. But guess what? What you open your eyes to is even worse: more monsters, more fear. Close your eyes, open them, close your eyes, open them. No respite. Identity is lost in that blink of an eye.

I had no identity; Dolly Sen was gone when I downed a packet of my dad's medication with a glass of water. There was only pain and torment to extinguish.

But I survived that attempt. I was violently sick and in a lot of abdominal pain for just over a day, but I didn't die.

And so the horror continued. I began to withdraw and refused to go to school, and social services became involved because of it. I was obviously just another case to them; they didn't really give a damn. They asked if I was having problems at home, with my dad, my abuser, sitting right next to me. Social workers only offered me more humiliation and brutalisation. Every time I saw a social worker, they had that look on their face saying, 'What now?' My body was a room, where my being was huddled in a corner. Social workers did nothing to draw me out; they only made me withdraw further. I'm wondering now: did I ever hear a compassionate, useful thing from them? Because all I can remember is, 'Go to school or we'll take you away from your family.' My teenage years was a place I learned there is no God, and life is as precious as your loneliness.

So on top of the psychosis, the abuse, the neglect, and indifference and collusion of authorities, I became severely depressed to the point of catatonia. Looking back, I am surprised that I didn't attempt suicide more times than I did.

The only thing I did was read, that was my sanctuary. In my early 20s I began to write too. Going over my first writings, you could see I was suicide-obsessed. Here is a sample of my writing from then: 'Thoughts of suicide were my alarm clock in those early hours – suicide was a comfortable bed – a sleep that actually slept – a sun that didn't burn you as it offered your lonely world light – well, that morning, I wanted death more than daytime TV. But my gun was in another room, far away, and as I am a lazy person, and as my cowardice has a beautiful star, I waited for the sun to rise instead … I am God inside the body of a nobody – but then again, aren't we all? These voices get my undivided attention. They dictate my suicide note to me on the most beautiful of days – poetic justice – they tear my mind apart; they rent out my mind to dead souls, dead souls that were happy to be dead … I feel mutilated by life, violated by living – the only high I want to be is six feet deep … To be tortured and tortured and tortured and not allowed to die – that's life for you, and it feels absolutely beautiful …'

Apart from my blossoming creativity, I found Buddhism, which helped me begin to challenge my negative thinking: the self-destructive thoughts lessened, but didn't go away. I thought about suicide 100 times a day rather than 1000 times. Some improvement I guess.

Fast-forward 10 years later: I was slowly, slowly improving things for myself. I was still in the mental health system, over-medicated, and self-harming occasionally, with a few psychiatric hospital admissions under my belt. But at the same time, I was making small steps to improve my life: I had my own flat, was doing voluntary work, and was beginning the healing process of forgiving my dad. I had just fallen in love with a woman. When our relationship collapsed, I became actively suicidal again. Apart from the extraordinary pain of an ordinary broken heart, the experience brought to the surface the deeply imbedded belief that I was unlovable, which started the domino effect of ever-darkening thoughts and the belief I was better off dead. When I told my care coordinator at the time I was going to kill myself, she referred me to the Home Treatment Team, who were going to visit me at home for an assessment.

Two men from the local Home Treatment Team knocked on my door and began by telling me that Home Treatment was for very ill people and that I did not fit the bill 'because my personal hygiene was good and my shoes were clean'! They continued to make basic false assumptions about mental health like that. They were **telling** me I was not suicidal when in fact I was. They said this because I wasn't crying. They didn't let me talk and I didn't want to confide anyway because you could see there was no way I could tell them anything. They had their minds already made up. They had an aggressive swagger about them, which scared me. I could just imagine them holding me down in my own home to inject medication into me. I was an old hand in the psychiatric game but their behaviour shocked even me. If I had been just in the first phases of mental distress and suicidalness and was hoping that the medical services could save me, and had what I just experienced as my first contact with mental

THE SUICIDE NOTE IS NOT MY STORY 139

health services, I would have waited till they left and committed suicide. But the best was still to come. I told them that I couldn't sleep and that I had just split up with my partner and it was very painful. One of them perked up and said, 'Well, kill two birds with one stone and read Mills & Boon at bedtime and you'll be fine.'

The hole the relationship break-up had left me with was shattering; I wanted to die and for him to be as blasé as that, I couldn't believe what I was hearing. What scared me was that I was totally vulnerable and they couldn't see that. Then he kept referring to my partner as he/him when I said it was a her. 'You're better off with a man anyway,' said one of them.

Home Treatment on paper is such a good idea in that people don't need to go into hospital. But if the same kind of staff is manning Home Treatment teams as inpatient wards, it just means being abused in your own home. I said to my care coordinator afterwards, 'If that is Home Treatment, I'd rather go into hospital.' I said that because I didn't want memories of being unsafe and traumatised in my own home. At least, in hospital, the association wouldn't be so personal once I got out.

What happened instead was I did get a kind of home treatment care plan but it wasn't peopled by Home Treatment! I had the workers of my Mental Health Centre in Streatham visit me or call me once a day to see how I was doing and to gauge my level of suicidal intent. Or I would go to the Centre to see someone. They were lovely. I was well looked after and I felt that they really cared for me and wanted the best for me. They tried to get me to go to the Women's Crisis House in Streatham instead of hospital. I went for an assessment there and didn't like the vibes of the place. It was cold, quiet and clinical even though homely decoration was the intent. I was interviewed by one of the therapists. There was just no warmth from this woman, just icy analysis of my whole personality in an hour interview. I declined the offer to stay there. I learned later that the Crisis House had three suicides in only its year-long history, and therefore subsequently closed down.

I can't sing my praises enough for how the staff of Streatham Mental Health treated me when I was at my most distressed. I was listened to, treated with respect, and spoken to like an equal, with a real genuine warmness. I remember one of them, when I told her about the Mills & Boon comment and homophobia of the Home Treatment guy, she said, 'Report the bastard!' Which gave me my first smile in weeks, for lots of reasons I guess: that she cared about me, that she wasn't homophobic, that she saw the mental health system needs improving, and didn't take sides with a fellow nurse.

Like being on the receiving side of racism and sexism, homophobia is a painful prejudice to experience. To be abused or alienated in a society will have an adverse effect on your mental health. How can it not? It attacks who you fundamentally are. Just imagine the devastating effect of coming out to your family as gay, bisexual or transgender and have them utterly reject you. You think: am I really that terrible, that unlovable, that my own parents hate me because of the gender of the person I love? So it is as no surprise that there are studies where it is recounted that anywhere between 20 and 50 per cent of LGBT people attempt suicide.

Each form of discrimination or prejudice has its own shape, and homophobia is unique in that prejudice can come from your own family, and in that way, is even more devastating.

It is hard also to be young and gay, especially if you don't have gay role models to help you through teenage landmarks that your straight counterparts take for granted like first crush, first kiss, first date, first sex, and so on. As non-straight people this is how we experience life and the mental health system. Every member of staff in the mental health system needs to understand this.

Luckily, although I had the awful experience with Home Treatment, I was lucky enough to get support elsewhere. But what if I hadn't?

If you give a suicidal person compassion, show them you care about them, and support them through difficult times, and offer them ways to help themselves; you will more than likely save their life. Because that was exactly what saved mine.

I personally think a minute of pure compassion is better than ten years on psychiatric meds. Because can a tablet cure abuse? Stigma? Loneliness? Self-hate? Compassion heals those. I have been grateful for the compassion of others, but one thing that was missing was compassion for self.

And that began with the writing of my first memoir, *The World is Full of Laughter,* published by Chipmunka in 2002. Writing was cathartic, but it was in reading my story where I felt empathy for myself for the first time. I realised that I was doing the best I could do, I was a survivor. That should be celebrated and not hated. In fact, I said of it: 'It started off a suicide note and ended a celebration of life.' It also gave me another gift: the understanding that I could write my life story the way I wanted. I had no choice in how the story started but I have a choice in how it ends. Ending it in suicide was my abusers writing my story. My father and the other abusers in my life couldn't even write a Pot Noodle commercial; why was I giving them power to still dictate my life? I can now choose the plot, the ending and the characters in it.

I will try and make it beautiful, even if there are characters in it who haunt me. Giving them minor roles has made my character bloom and flourish.

I have made huge positive strides in my life, but has suicide lost its seduction? No, I still think about it daily. We live in harsh, cynical times, where meaninglessness and pain are the ghosts that haunt our times, and I sometimes feel hopeless about myself and the world around me. But one of my saving graces is my sense of humour. If I can't laugh at my pain – because, let's face it, being human is an absurd, ridiculous career – then what I do is look at light, inside myself or outside myself. Or I try to create more light: in compassionate acts to others or to the world or to myself; or in an act of creativity, which gives me the power to paint a sun over the darkest nights, to turn suicide notes into songs.

I am not ashamed of my suicidal pain or attempts. I am a sensitive person who went through extreme trauma. For many years I punished myself and felt ashamed of my sensitivity, but now I know sensitivity is one of my strengths. Sensitivity is not a weakness; it is the world that is messed up. It is the reason why I am compassionate to others. It is the reason why beauty and nature and love can move me to tears. That is an immense gift.

No one can escape pain. Nor can anyone escape the ability to learn from the pain. I am still growing. I still believe in my own light. Always believe there is light at the end of the tunnel. There has to be because you are the light. Even when you want to shut down that light and everything seems dark, something shines. It might be a tiny spark buried in an eternity of darkness, but the spark is still there to be seen, it can't be hidden. It is not in its job description to be hidden. I am not minimising the impact of childhood abuse, but the way I look at it is: if you had childhood abuse or any kind of severe trauma, it's an obligation to give that hurt child or person the right to be the human they would have been; it's an obligation to your dreams and your freedom to be. So I feed my spirit, and give that child reasons to celebrate life, until the shape of my heart and soul grows so big, it can never shrink again.

Learning/discussion points:

- If someone says they are suicidal, don't ever say they are not, or trivialise their distress. That is the worst thing you can do. Acknowledge their upset and work together to find ways forward.

- If you haven't already, get some training around how to work with LGBT (lesbian, gay, bisexual, transsexual) service users. The anxiety, depression, suicidality or substance misuse of some LGBT service users may be compounded by societal and institutional homophobia. The less homophobia in mental health services, the better the trust and prospects of recovery for those users.

Phoenix to ashes

25

Madame de Merteuil

Those who have not been in that darkest of all places will never understand. However much we write or tell, those who read us or listen to us will always be able to reduce our experience to 'drama', 'exaggeration', 'manipulation', even 'lie'.

To really understand, one must have walked through that darkness and come through. I am not sure my words will enlighten anyone, but I certainly hope they will be a step on the way, for there is a very pressing need to change our societal attitude to suicide. There is a need to make others see those who suffer in silence, a need to make their silent scream heard.

So, here is my story. A story of a woman walking the path of self-destruction, near annihilation and rebirth.

Like many, I had an ordinary life. Looking at me from the outside, one would have thought I was doing rather well: I had what is called 'a good job' in the city of London, programming software for banks, and a bunch of cool friends to party with during the weekends. I was 30. At the start of that all-important decade of life where one is still full of the energy of youth whilst having acquired that little pinch of wisdom that comes from having lived independently.

My life could have been at its apex. But it wasn't. All the parameters were wrong. Never judge a book by its cover. The 'good job' was a trap, enslaving me to 50-plus hours a week in an environment where presenteeism was king and all individuality had to be erased. Always wear the expected suit, always turn up at the precise expected time, always with the expected company attitude. Stay long hours, it's expected. If you don't, you'll get an email reminding you that people notice that you've left one minute too early.

You barely have the time to think. But in those few moments where my personality could get a word in, it was screaming, 'This is wrong, this is not making you grow, this is only putting food on the table and paying the mortgage. This is not living, this is existing.' I was feeling trapped, like a hamster in a wheel, unable to come off.

In order to justify the sacrifice of my individuality to a soulless job, I decided to throw myself into endless partying at weekends, thinking I was expressing myself for at least two days a week. I was burning the candle at both ends. Traditional tale? One doesn't realise what is really going on until it's too late.

It was New Year's Eve. I was at a party. One more party, wearing the funky clothes the soulless job paid for. Thinking that at least I was using the money to dress the way I wanted on that day, to be who I really was. But then it suddenly dawned on me. I wasn't being who I really was at all. I was just escaping, I was just trying to not think that my life made no sense, I was just … acting.

That sudden realisation projected me into another dimension. I was suddenly watching my life from the outside, seeing it in all its meaninglessness, its emptiness, its lack of self-actualisation. Was this living? Was this worth it? Not, it wasn't. I was wasting my time. Drained of all energy as I was, I didn't just sit down and decide to live differently. Maybe I would have if someone had listened to me at that party when I started to sob uncontrollably, needing a shoulder to lean on, a little bit of humanity, five minutes of warmth.

But everybody else was just in their bubble of amusement, unable to connect with my despair, afraid of the void my distress was revealing. Maybe it was their instinct telling them that: should they stop and listen to me, they would understand that my meaningless life was the mirror of their own emptiness. They couldn't allow that to happen. Everyone has a survival instinct. In the face of danger, flight.

So, in order to not have to confront their own disillusions mirrored in mine, all the other people at the party brushed me off with the usual 'Come on, pick yourself up' or 'Don't bring the mood down'.

I was left alone in my despair and, inevitably, the darkness grew. I was now feeling not only trapped in an absurd life, but unloved and rejected by others. My 'friends' were no friends at all.

I left the party in a cab, like an automaton, and went home straight to my medicine cabinet and mechanically crushed all the pills together and put them in a litre of vodka. There were a lot of benzodiazepines there, obtained from the Internet. They had been helping me cope with my empty existence. Now they would help me put an end to it.

I crushed quantities of Xanax and Diazepam together. Once dissolved into powder, I put them into the vodka and mixed the lot with orange juice. Don't ask me why I was bothered with making the drink taste better. I was in a daze. Remembering it now, it is almost as if I had dissociated from life so much that I was automatically performing gesture to end my existence and watching myself do it. I recall calculating that there were enough pills to kill a man of 90 kilograms. I even researched the fact on the Internet. All my actions were mechanical, cold, calculated, with the only goal of destroying myself. But I didn't think of me as 'myself'. I was thinking of me as 'that body to destroy'.

So, I was sure I was going to succeed. Yes, succeed. When you're suicidal, death is your goal so achieving it is success.

I drank the whole vodka, crushed pills and orange juice. I remember lying on my sofa, sliding into unconsciousness, thinking it was over at last and nobody would care anyway. If they did, they would have given me a few minutes at that party, right? I do not know how long it had been when I vaguely woke up, with extremely painful contractions in my belly and being sick. In my pain, I jerked and fell off the sofa.

I was violently sick and collapsed again. I woke up God knows how long after, thinking 'Oh no, I'm still alive. I've failed. I've failed at dying as I've failed at living. Can't I do anything right. Can't I be given the chance to at least end it?'

Reading this, you may think that I was being selfish, considering only my point of view, not taking one minute to consider the consequences on my family or other loved ones. Truth is, when that darkness has you, you do not relate to anything that is life anymore. You see yourself as a piece of meat to destroy; you cannot even start to see the bigger picture of your connections, the people whom your death could impact. It's emptiness and complete absence of humanity. Utter loneliness and despair. I do not know if I have the words to describe it, as it has now been a long time and, looking back, the whole chain of events almost feels unreal. I was probably dead inside even if living on the outside.

It would take a long time for me to wake up and start feeling alive again. The scarier part is, even after therapy and recovery, I would try again.

Because nobody around me understood. Before I tried to commit suicide the second time, I told my friends I was considering it. I was trying to reach out, trying to get help. Maybe I was hoping that opening up to people I had helped with their own life struggles would get me out of the dark. I couldn't have been more wrong. I was told I was being manipulative and a lying drama queen. That is the very thing that pushed me to do the deed for the second time.

This time it was with other substances. But the same 'scientific' research came into it. And the same miraculous physical resistance intervened. Again, I didn't die. Again, I felt cheated and didn't understand why.

Now, looking back, I know that darkness is still within me and threatens me every day. I know I have to contain it. I know I have to find meaning to my existence and keep good company or I will walk the path of self-destruction again.

I envy those of you who do not suffer this. Ignorance is bliss. Maybe you are lucky enough to have a job that feeds your soul, or loved ones who truly love you. I am still looking for the career but at least I have found the people. For the time being, things are much better. But I am always afraid I will be triggered into self-destructing mode again. Life is full of those events which can make one think there isn't any meaning, that the duties of surviving overtake self-actualisation, that people do not really see us.

But then again, there are those beautiful, simple moments of joy: a sunny day, a beautiful piece of art, an interesting book, a smile from a loved one. I have learned to cherish those moments and I try to remember them when I feel the darkness rise in me again. For if the force that could destroy me is within me, the force that can save me also is. That is what we learn when we confront utter despair. We can rise again, like the phoenix from the ashes.

26

The day I went to the meadow

Felicity Stennett

I sat there in the kitchen. A bread knife in my hand. Repeatedly I sliced and sliced at my wrist but felt nothing. A text message brought me out of what I was to learn was dissociation. This was happening often. There would be times of confusion where I couldn't figure out what I'd done, but the scars revealed all.

I was soon introduced to the psychiatric team and admitted onto a psychiatric ward.

I sat on my bed alone one night. Blade in my hand, unsure of what the consequence would be but I knew too well that I would soon find out. Having learnt how to take blood in my training I was confident I could find a vein and simply bleed out. I'd found the vein and felt it spasm all the way down my scarred arm as I attacked it with a blade. Gosh it hurt and it wasn't bleeding. I stopped feeling defeated, tired and frustrated. During the night I was awoken by a feeling of wetness and was alarmed to see blood all over my bed and the floor. Without thinking I pressed my buzzer and a nurse encouraged me to apply pressure. The second she left I let it bleed. It spurted everywhere and I was in a trance watching it flow so fast. The nurse returned and snapped me out of it and stopped the bleeding.

I had never in my life felt so calm and peaceful. All my troubles had disappeared, as I was too exhausted from the vast loss of blood to think about everything that was troubling me.

I began to crave this intense calming feeling. Initially it was a method of survival. A way to protect myself from all the hurt and trauma I was reliving in my head. Worries of the past, the future; even simple things like deciding whether to have tea or coffee became too overwhelming. My brain was so full it couldn't hold any more.

The blood-letting became more common and more dangerous. I got a buzz out of putting my life on the edge and making fate decide whether I lived or died. Each episode resulted in higher volumes of blood loss.

The constant blood loss encouraged my body to over-clot, which ultimately has put my life in serious danger. I was no longer in charge of my body. The clots had taken over and my loss of control was too much to deal with. I had to take the control back. It was my body; I chose when to be ill. Being placed on blood thinners was a big mistake. I saw it as a get out, a way to escape this wasteful life and be free from the vile thoughts in my head. I'd prepared for my death anyway due to the poor diagnosis I had which was caused by the clots. I had written birthday cards for my son up to his 18th birthday and sought legal advice about a will. I couldn't cope any longer. I couldn't process simple information.

I had many things whirling around in my head: my poor health, my husband's poor health, my phobia of people and social situations. I'd managed to convince myself that I was no good for my son; our inability to conceive was a stress; the memories from my childhood abuse and the way that my parents were treating me. It was all more than I could take.

I had changed as a person. I wasn't frightened of anything or anyone. Nothing or no one could hurt me more than I already had been. I became more angry. Arguing with people whereas before I wouldn't dare. I had also got myself into two fights, whereas before I wouldn't dream of violence, I wouldn't want to hurt anyone and used to be frightened of people hurting me. But suddenly I stopped caring.

I felt heartbroken that my parents would happily erase me from their life. I hadn't spoken to them for two months. They thought I had brought shame on the family by reporting to the police that I'd been sexually abused by somebody I knew. I had done nothing wrong. I simply wanted closure but the police couldn't prove anything and the case was dropped. I was so alone. I felt like the black sheep of the family. The rejection and lack of acknowledgement from my parents was enough to push me over the edge. My head felt like it was going to explode. Existing wasn't enough anymore. Don't get me wrong. I had tried to survive, tried to get better. I had been through a year's worth of dialectal behavioural therapy (DBT) but still found no way of managing to be alive. This was the day. I woke up and the day was a blur just waiting for the right time. I had no problem finding my vein as I had repeatedly attacked the same place in my arm and it never failed to relieve me by gushing blood. I placed towels on the floor and sat and bled. The faster the blood escaped my body the quicker I was relieved. I sat there thinking 'I really should stop – I am actually going to kill myself, is that what I really, truly want?' I couldn't stop. I didn't want to and I couldn't if I did. The blood was flowing so fast. I could feel myself getting weaker and weaker and enjoying every nanosecond of intense calm; this was it. But it wasn't. The door flew open. I couldn't keep my eyes open long enough to see what was happening. The next thing I knew paramedics were lifting me onto a trolley. Then I'd gone. I was so happy and elated. I was in a meadow full of beautiful flowers, trees, butterflies and children happily skipping and singing. The sun shone and it was the most stunning place I had ever seen, I never wanted to leave this wonderful place. Suddenly, something didn't seem right. I was in this wonderful place full of beauty, freedom and happiness yet someone was aggressively calling my name. Each time it was more aggressive and violent and I needed to find out why this was happening. It didn't fit in with my meadow. I slowly awoke surrounded by doctors, nurses, people trying to cannulate me in every limb.

'I DON'T WANT BLOOD!' I managed to scream. I wanted to go back to my meadow. In and out of consciousness, I was so tired but every now and then I would awake and try to remove the needles, wires, oxygen, anything I could get hold of, but I wasn't strong enough and quickly fell unconscious again. After two hours I came round and realised that I had yet again escaped death. I was angry because I knew I would be in this situation again. They wanted to give me two more units of blood but I refused.

I continue to be in a life-or-death situation. I can't even begin to imagine living a happy life. My demands of life have reduced. All I want is to be a good mother and a good wife, but the tornado in my head won't allow that.

The pull to cutting and putting my life on edge is too appealing. Do I want to die? Yes. No. I don't know. I genuinely believe that this world can't provide me with the happiness that I thought it once could. I have little value for my life and continue to put it at risk.

Some people are lucky enough to get through life happily with minor struggles along the way. They don't see the people that are struggling to live; every breath is emotionally painful. We were brought into this world to be abused, mistreated, let down, neglected, hurt to the point where we hurt ourselves. Yes love is offered, friendships are offered, but having been hurt too many times we stay away from close relationships. We trust no one. As a borderline I can empathise with those of the same diagnosis but I know that no matter how hard I try, I cannot save them from the mental torture they experience, as no one can save me. We can only save ourselves but it is easier to give in to the pull of death.

27

'Con Hearse'

Kathryn

It wasn't until he started beckoning for all the other shop assistants to come over and marvel at the amazing, death-defying experience that I had just shared with the young, fit, outdoorsy-type salesman that I began to feel sick.

Just as my story of jumping from an aircraft at over 600 feet over the Pyrenees, and the parachute failing to open as I crashed at great speed to the floor, had seemed too watertight – it now seemed to have holes that were so big that anyone over the age of five could have fitted into them.

Martin and I had joked about the different stories we could come up with to explain the anomaly; we had produced a list of no less than 27 different explanations as to why my body was so fucked up. The aeroplane/parachute story was never my favourite and I knew why. Firstly, I had never jumped out of a plane in any circumstances and if you are going to lie about something then the general rule is that you have done some pretty good research. Secondly, I didn't even know off the top of my head where the Pyrenees were – so not only had this lie not been thought through properly, it had been based on the assumption that no one should ask me anything. And finally, if I had indeed fallen 600 feet then I would definitely not be standing in a shop trying to purchase footwear – as I would be more likely to be sitting in a brown-coloured urn on top of my mother's fire surround.

Just as I was crap at trying to kill myself, I was also crap about lying, especially about this. It would have only taken someone with the slightest bit of medical knowledge to have realised that you don't get pancake feet from having a car crash or being bashed onto a rock in a winter storm in the Mediterranean, and most certainly not from falling out of a plane. It was a shit lie and I knew it and just as easy as it was lying in bed in hospital coming up with mad stories with Martin, a cheeky guy I had met on the ward, putting them into practice in the real world was not so easy.

I was trying to buy a pair of shoes. In one respect I was extremely lucky that I had thrown myself off a building at a time when comfortable, flat, broad footwear was the in-thing. If it hadn't have been I would have been forced to design an entire new range of shoes and called them 'Jumpers' for the over-45s who desire style, comfort and modesty but with the extra thick soles just in case Atos* find them 'fit for work' and they need to try killing themselves twice; 'Crush Puppies' for the 60+ suicide attempter wanting that fashion appeal with extra width and soft leather; 'Con Hearse' for the younger mental health patient wanting suicide with style; and 'Step Offs' for those summer evenings that suit all ages. Thankfully, I had no need to concern myself with a new designer range to meet the needs of those 'awkward to fit' feet on people who jump off tall buildings as this was the 20th century, an age where all 'crankpots' could be catered for in the world of feet, where women need not suffer in seven inch, strappy, patent leather stilettos any more, for they craved comfort and style, and Crocs, FitFlops, Cloggs and Ugg were queuing up to provide for everyone with feet all shapes and sizes without looking like a geek, even for those who have been left with pancake feet, battered by hitting the concrete at a hundred miles an hour.

I decided to leave the shop to the people who could walk more than a few feet and instead shop on the Internet to avoid any more uncomfortable situations that only served the purpose of making me look a total idiot.

In the first couple of years, my contact with the outside world was limited. Apart from my own friendship circles, the local Co-op and the checkout staff at Asda, I avoided public contact with anyone other than those who were paying me to tell them my story or for educational purposes only. I struggled with coming to terms very much with what I had done and the impact this was having on all aspects of my life. It's such an odd thing to say to people, 'Hi, I'm Kathryn, I threw myself off a building, how are you?' Somehow it doesn't seem to flow as smoothly as 'Hi, I'm Kathryn, I have cancer' or 'Hi, I'm Kathryn, I have been in a car crash on the M1', another lie that always seems to evoke a response of 'Was it your fault?', presuming that they are checking out whether I

---

* Atos Healthcare carries out disability assessments on behalf of the Department for Work and Pensions (DWP).

have received an adequate amount of compensation for my misfortune. One thing was for sure, it was never a good chat-up line.

In the beginning, when I was much slimmer, the perfect diet plan always being put into a coma, the unfortunate event had earned me some cool, rock and roll 'hot to trot' points in certain, dark, alternative circles. A freak sex object, where scary men want weird sex with women wearing pots and bags and other medical appliances attached. In fact, my increased ability to pull had certainly not gone unnoticed and it wasn't long before female peers began to show signs of jealously and even consider making the leap themselves.

In the first six weeks after being discharged I had more male attention than I had had for years. Just like 'normal' women were draped in their gold jewellery, I was donning new, state-of-the-art hospital wear. With sexy black pots to my knees, a colostomy bag and skin that looked like I was an Ed Gein victim that he had got bored with halfway through slashing. I wined and dined in my super wheelchair. For the more straight folk on the planet it was met with surprise, shock, anger and sometimes, more often, fear.

In actual fact, agonising over what people knew or didn't know about the incident was fairly futile. Following discharge from the orthopaedic ward, I had a team of mental health professionals involved in my care. They were doing a great job of spreading the word to their own family and friends, who in turn spread that word to their extended family and friends and by the law of the six degrees of separation it wasn't too long before it got back to me. Upon realising that the story was in fact mine, and only mine to tell, I boarded the express locomotive to mental health survivor training. Just like they were getting paid to spread my muck, so now was I.

However, the appropriateness of telling people the truth about my little 'incident' was to be a continuing theme. Later down the line, resigned to adopting a slightly more sensible, realistic approach (for economic reasons only), and the fact that I also began to get bored hearing my own voice repeatedly telling the hilarious but equally uncomfortable and upsetting story, careful thought and revision were needed when it came to imparting this information.

Not everyone had the stomach to deal with such a 'heinous crime' against oneself. Not everyone would understand that people do not throw themselves off buildings unless they are seriously unwell, just like cancer. Some even thought that it was an outrage. Like I had done it for fun or was particularly bored that day. 'Oh, what shall I do today? Telly is crap, no one wants to go out for a drink – I know, I'll throw myself off a very tall building.' It did make me wonder what I should do with myself now, given I offend some people so much? 'Did you not think about your daughter?' or 'How selfish of you to do that' were a few comments that were regularly made. How could I stop being so offensive? Should I consider another suicide attempt? Should I leave all my friends and family again and move to a remote part of the world where no one would have to look at me again? What should I have done?

A few years after my 'offensive' act, my close childhood friend's mother tragically took her own life by drowning, on a cruel winter's night in December. Coincidentally she also had a diagnosis of bipolar disorder and had suffered many desperate and torturous years, battling with the savage effects of chronic mental ill health.

Hundreds flocked to City Road Cemetery on that day to pay their respects where they were told in no uncertain terms by Catherine, who stood so boldly and courageously, that 'MY MUM WAS ILL, JUST LIKE SOMEONE WITH CANCER', which was a profound and deeply chilling speech served up with a cocktail of anger, grief and shock. Despite me knowing that both her mother and I had been so very ill and despite me knowing that neither incident was personally against anyone and not designed in any way to cause the maximum damage to our loved ones, for the rest of their lives, I stood there feeling as if I had murdered someone – as if I was guilty, not just for the 'crime' against myself that I had committed, but also hers, for I knew more than anyone else in that room, in that moment, on that day, that I was the only one with a level of understanding about what could have been going through my friend's mother's mind in that moment.

The funeral itself left me with a bitter taste in my mouth. I looked round at the crowds and wondered what many of those present actually truly felt. Did they all come because they knew and loved her, did they come because they had empathy and understanding for the violent act she had committed against herself, or did they come for a bit of 'voyeurism'? I knew all too well what that looked like from my time in hospital. The rubbernecking associates, imitating compassion and identification with the abnormal spread out in front of them. How much did these people really care? How many minutes of their own lives did they give up to show warmth and understanding before the tragic event?

I quietly considered the façade of our daily lives where most intimates exchange disingenuous, deceptive pleasantries, as it is human nature to hurt, betray and deceive the very people we weep into Kleenex for when they lie before us in a wooden casket, when they are gone from this world forever. The adverts posted on social networks, 'Mental illness affects one in four', 'Spend a little time with someone who is suffering', are so meaningless as anyone would tell you that to spend time with someone who is so ill they are wanting to 'end it all' is not an easy or a very comfortable thing to do. I thought about my own funeral and whether the people who shunned me after coming out of hospital would have indeed been standing in a room like this weeping in the same way this crowd was, placing their hands on my own child's shoulder in a gesture of 'heartfelt sympathy'.

Whether the same people in my community who shut their curtains as I wheeled myself up the road in my Neanderthal hospital chair and the people who I thought were my friends, people who I had worked with in social work, the very profession itself professing to be 'non-judgemental', metamorphosed into fickle and untrustworthy individuals would have been stood there, feigning grief whilst satisfying a mis-represented need to mourn their own failures in that hour of darkness we all shall face one day. The bottom line was that I didn't care, I had humour and I was going to use my gift of 'the Laugh' to get through this complex, deep and disturbing situation. If I was going to make a difference to anything and change attitudes, it certainly wasn't by being angry. A clever combination of openness and the power of 'the Laugh' moved mountains in helping to explain the illogical, the absurd and the inexplicable.

As the months progressed, so did the fear of losing my legs. There were two plus points to this event taking place – one being that I would never have to shop for shoes again – the other being that I would definitely be in for a healthy shot at the 'Slimmer of the Week Award'. The infection caused by the equipment used to save my feet now might be the reason for losing them, the ultimate price to pay. But this was my cross to bear and mine only. The permanence I would carry on my shoulders for the rest of my life. I didn't care, for I was alive, I was here too for my family and I was here for my friends, the only things that mattered. For me, contrary to what others were thinking and feeling about me, my own life was looking fairly good.

People, who had been holding it together for me, keeping their emotions intact and strong, began to spill over. I didn't feel quite ready for this, not ready to hear their experiences from their side of things, things I could know little about despite me being physically present in the world. I had been anaesthetised, saved from the trauma of other people's hurt, their intense grief, while the doctors battled to save my life. This was an inevitable procedure, an uncomfortable but necessary unburdening of the truth, advanced whether I wanted it or not; it was my time to listen. The chapter in the story I could not and did not wish to erase was other people's experiences of the same event.

Their silent commitment through the darkest months had left differing but equally disturbing emotional scarring on my 'inner circle'. It was their time to heal, their time to impart the story of their journey to me. Some found this harder than others. Those who had had experiences of losing their loved one, their primary carer as a child, their lover or their friend, whether through suicide, natural causes or foul play, transferred anger and confusion towards me. Others were just plain shocked, bewildered and frightened. I felt a desperate sense of blame for the plethora of feeling, experiences and past hurts, a sense of blame I couldn't allow to get into my psyche to prevent me from maintaining the positive stance I had adopted, designed to protect, heal and ultimately rebuild.

So the lying and being economical with the truth will continue for as long as I live. A complex conundrum necessary for protecting both myself and others. Just as the power of 'the Laugh' helps to change attitudes, the increase of ignorance and hate, fuelled by government and media, towards people with mental illness and disability continues. Just as there will always be people who love and accept me, there will always be those who don't. There will always be those who will never accept my experiences but I have the quiet knowledge that one day, they too will have an experience that other people find difficult, which may well help them to have more empathy. There will also always be those who I am afraid to tell, as I think it is too much for some people to take on board. I am in contact with many people who have a learning disability and I am surrounded by children in my private life. I work with disabled people and their carers who are often in extremely distressing situations themselves, and I recognise that although this is a part of me I do not wish to deny and that I own my experiences and am proud of myself for being so open, not everyone should know. I will continue with care, to judge the appropriateness of sharing 'my' information both in work and in my private life.

28

'The Silence of Suicide'

Michael Skinner

I would like to open up my thoughts and feelings in regards to 'The Silence of Suicide' by first sharing the lyrics to a song that I wrote several years ago that deals

with the losses of loved ones and friends to suicide – these words also have meaning for me in regards to my own struggles and surviving several suicide attempts.

FOLLOW THE LIGHT*

VERSE 1
It's another dark ... lonely night
Sitting all alone ... he can't see the light
All alone with these thoughts ... there's so much pain
All of these dark thoughts – they're driving him insane

CHORUS
If I could only take back time
I wish you didn't take your life
If I only could of erased your pain
To see your face once again
All I can say is follow the light
Oh dear brother, follow the light

VERSE 2
Sitting by herself ... and it starts to rain
She feels so alone ... she can't stop the pain
Unresolved tears ... she's drowning in shame
All of these dark thoughts – they're driving her insane

---

* © Michael Skinner Music, www.mskinnermusic.com, mikeskinner@comcast.net

CHORUS

If I could only take back time
I wish you didn't take your life
Your pretty smile hid the pain
I thought I'd see you again
Now we can't sing our songs
I find the ways to carry on
I hope that you followed the light
Oh dear girl follow the light
Please follow the light
Please follow that light

LEAD BREAK

CHORUS

If I could only take back time
I wish you didn't take your life
No one understood your pain
So many just turned away
While you drowned in the rain
Drowning sorrows of black rain
And I can't take back time
So just follow the light
Please follow the light
Please follow that light

Suicide – such a dark and powerful word and all that it conjures up. This word has had a deep and profound impact upon my own life in so many ways and

for those I love and care for. It is my desire that my personal experiences of suicide can offer hope, healing and understanding around these complex issues and

help people to re-think some of the misconceptions, stigma and discrimination associated with suicide.

This song of mine, *Follow the Light*, was a work in progress for so many years – even before the lyrics and music came together back in November and

December of 2006. I think that it took a long time for this tune to come to fruition and express my feelings because of the deep dark pain I felt inside and my own denial and avoidance of those feelings and all that it entailed. Through this song I was able to share some of my deepest thoughts and feelings over the loss of two

brothers and two friends to suicide. Sadness and grief can be a very difficult journey to embark upon – especially when we get the signals and the message from

the greater part of society that we need to move on with our lives – to just '*get over it*'. How do we just get over it when loss, sadness and grief are such difficult

subjects to deal with? Sadly, for so many of us who are impacted by suicide, we learn that the feelings we so desperately need to work through are not welcomed

by others. The mindset of so many is to just shut it down and act like all is well. This becomes even more confusing and complicated when dealing with the pain

and sorrow of suicide – a word that most people don't want to hear about, much less talk about it.

There are many reasons why I shut down my own feelings associated with the loss of my brothers David and Danny and my friends. Avoidance, denial and fear

come to mind in why it took me so long to finally address the grief, the sadness and the losses I experienced, not to mention the fear of working through my own

pain and sorrow from my suicide attempts and the deep-held shame that I felt because of those experiences.

As a child growing up in a very abusive home, one learned very quickly that feelings were not allowed to be shown and expressed in any manner whatsoever.

The simple statement of, '*I'll give you something to cry about*' took on whole new dimensions when living in a house of horror – a house of pain, sadness and

sheer terror. As a young boy of eight or nine years old, the message was driven home front and center in clear understandable terms – one could not express

oneself in any way, shape or form. The suicide attempt of my mother back then only reinforced this. Nothing was said or done, yet we knew, at least I knew that something was terribly wrong because of her being away in the hospital for several days and when she came home both of her wrists were heavily bandaged.

I can only remember snippets of what was said back then – of how she had almost died because of the huge loss of blood. I can remember one night tossing and

turning in bed and hearing my father quietly sobbing in the other room. This was indeed a rare event in the history of my life as he never showed any emotions such

as sorrow in front of us. The early message of silence was deeply reinforced by the actions around my mother's suicide attempt.

This became even more complicated and confusing for me as a young boy because my mother and father were responsible for so much of the pain and suffering

inflicted upon my siblings and me. It's difficult for many people to imagine that there are parents who see their very young children as a sexual commodity to be

used and even shared with other perverts – parents who seem incapable of compassion and empathy. My emotions were so damn confusing – I wanted to see

them dead, I was even thinking of ways I could kill them. Something is terribly wrong when a child has these feelings about his parents. I wrestled with so much

guilt back then because part of me wanted her to die. No child should have to contend with such powerfully disturbing thoughts and feelings about their parents.

My two siblings had both served in the military, one in the Air Force and one in the Army; they were fortunate to have never known combat during their time in the

service. Sadly, their war time was spent during their childhood and teenaged years. My two friends who succumbed to suicide also knew severe trauma and abuse

as young people. It is so hard to get the help one needs when devastated by child abuse. Rather than finding an empathic professional to witness the account of

our childhood trauma and offer support, many of us are instead given a label of some form of mental illness. Unfortunately, far too many people do not want to

address what drives so many to take their own life. I have a hard time to this day in talking about the child abuse so many of us have known, and when you add the

thoughts, attempts or losses of suicide into the mix, it has a way of sucking the oxygen out of the room and most people just turn away.

I don't believe that child abuse is the sole cause of suicide. But I do know from personal experience it is often fueled by what happened in childhood. There are all

kinds of losses, trauma and sorrow that can push someone to the brink of suicide, this I know to be true. Regardless of where it comes from, this deep dark desire

to end one's life is something that we need to be able to talk about as a community in a place of comfort, caring and safety.

> *Let people tell their story, tell of their pain. And let others listen. We discovered that in telling, that people begin to experience a healing.* (Archbishop Desmond Tutu)

We must be able to embrace, support and care for those so deeply hurt and wounded in life. When someone is mired in the deepest darkness of despair, the

thoughts and feelings of love and light can be so hard to comprehend. I know those disturbing and despondent thoughts – I would be remiss if I did not share of

my own depths of despair and how it brought me to have several attempts with intent to take my own life. Words cannot adequately describe how grateful and

fortunate I am to be here today – to be alive and be able to share of how I survived and found a way through the darkness of suicide.

Suicide and any thoughts about it were always anathema to me – it was not in my mindset. I have always been too determined and driven to be beaten down

by anything or anyone. I always likened myself to the Energizer Bunny that never stops, or compared myself to the old Timex watch commercials of '*It takes a*

licking and keeps on ticking'. That is not to say I never felt sad, lonely and depressed, but I always bounced back. I could be beaten down and knocked about

by so much in my life and from others and I may have been bent, but I was not broken. This mindset helped to keep me going for most of my life. I was successful

in pursuing my dreams and aspirations to become a professional musician. I even had the good fortune to live in and perform throughout Great Britain for two

years, drumming with the hard rock band, 'American Train'. I was also happily married and had the blessings of five of the greatest gifts of my life – my daughters.

And I had found success in life as a homeowner and business owner. My business kept me involved in music as a manager and booking agent while still being able

to perform as a drummer. All of these successes soon took a back seat in January of 1993 when I could no longer keep buried the sick secrets of my childhood

abuse. I had a nervous breakdown – I never want to go through such a horrendous nightmare again.

I now see my breakdown as a *breakthrough* – but back then, that was the farthest thing from my mind because I was overwhelmed with flashbacks from

complex post-traumatic stress, and I had major depression and was unable to work. I lost the business I had worked so hard to build. I even lost the ability to

play the drums for a few years. Those losses coupled with the abandonment of so many childhood friends and business associates also had a profound effect upon

my mental state. Mired in this place of deep despair and confusion I felt I was no good, I was tainted, I was damaged goods and I was 'mentally ill'. The

Energizer Bunny had run out of juice, the batteries had been drained and the Timex watch had been broken.

I could see that all of this was having a profound impact upon my wife and our daughters. That only brought on more guilt feelings and sorrow because I blamed myself for everything that was going on. It didn't help me to cope with these feelings and thoughts when the majority of the mental health treatment providers told

me repeatedly of how I was 'mentally ill' and this would be my lifetime of reality – this was as good as it gets.

Unfortunately, I could see that my wife was also now embracing the mindset that I was damaged beyond repair and a lifetime of 'mental illness' was all I would

know. Sadly, this belief system soon trickled down to our daughters, especially the three oldest teenagers. I knew they were frustrated, sad, angry, and confused,

and many of their feelings were justified and were normal reactions to an abnormal set of circumstances. I began to bear the brunt of my wife's and three oldest

daughters' frustration and sadness and that soon gave way to hostility and contempt for me as a person. I was no longer the husband and father but a thing to be

despised. They had no regard for me as a person and acted as if they had forgotten what I had once meant to them. I was weak in their eyes and it was all my

fault. They had bought into the belief held by so many in society that one needs to simply 'move on', 'get over it', that 'it was all in the past' and self-will and

determination would return me to good health – ha, if it were only that simple.

My life was such a struggle back then. My mind was so clouded and confused. I have never taken any illegal drugs of any kind throughout my life for I had seen

the dire consequences they had upon others and now I was prescribed a cocktail of drugs to 'help me', but they only made things worse. The drugs kept me

sedated, numb, and confused and in that state of mind came the distorted belief that my wife, our children and the world would be better off without me. I wanted

out because I felt that I had let my family down – those who I loved and cherished the most, those who once looked upon with me with deep respect and love.

Surely their lives would improve without me.

It was very late at night and I had ingested a vast amount of the drugs that had been over-prescribed to me. Shortly thereafter I called my brother Wayne to

apologize to him because I felt I was not supportive enough for him back when he was severely depressed. He could tell something was wrong and I let him

know that I would be leaving soon. Wayne called the emergency hotline and soon the ambulance and the police were at my home taking me to the hospital. That

I am here today to write this is indeed a miracle for me and not something to be taken lightly. I can remember my poor, bewildered wife visiting me at the hospital,

numb from it all, telling me how the doctor had told her that *my suicide actions were not a cry for help – it was intent to end my life, not an attempt.*

I did bounce back from that suicide intent and my wife was the one who now was convinced that the drugs were playing havoc with me – '*because this is not*

the man I know'. They only switched me onto other drugs; her words of concern and mine fell on deaf ears.

Sadly, my marriage had deteriorated. My wife lost hope in me and felt that I was broken and would never mend despite my attempts to convince her otherwise.

Her justifiable sadness, frustration, grief and anger soon manifested itself into darker forms of contempt and rage directed at me. There are many reasons why this

came to pass; her issues of depression, anxiety and child abuse had a profound impact in all of this. But it was easier to deflect and deny those aspects of her own

life and castigate me as the reason why everything was gone from us; she let me know on more than one occasion that '*you ruin everything*'. I had become the

scapegoat, the person to blame for all of her troubles in life. She only reinforced what I had been feeling all along since childhood that I was unworthy and unlovable.

My three oldest teenagers, encouraged by their mother, now voiced their contempt, frustration and anger at me. This only became worse during the divorce years

and soon they were alienated from me. That is still the deepest and most profound loss and hurt I have ever experienced – all of my childhood trauma and abuse

pales in comparison to the separation and loss of love from my children.

Once again there would be a serious suicide attempt fueled by alcohol and the prescriptions given to me. And yes, another phone call to say goodbye – this time

to the therapist who I do feel was helping me. She too suspected something was amiss, so once again came the drill of the ambulance, police, and the hospital.

Part of me felt relieved and glad to be alive … but full of deep shame for doing this again; and there was also a part of me that wished I had succeeded. I know

these are twisted and messed-up thoughts to have, but that was my reality – I had lost all hope. When you lose hope, you lose everything.

I tried so hard to look at my life with gratitude; I could see I still had some good friends who stuck by me and that meant so much, but I still felt so horrible and

confused inside, nothing was making sense. Sadly, there would be one more attempt at ending my life. The despair over the loss of my children consumed me. I

was devastated to my core – I had learned to love because of my children and now they were gone.

My third serious attempt on taking my life found me once again in a deep dark pool of sadness and grief; I was in so much pain, I had even taken out a hunting

knife and was cutting my wrists and knees, not to sever the arteries, but to numb the pain I was feeling … this only made me feel deeply ashamed, so I drank more

beer, unplugged the phone and sat sobbing over my losses in life. I took so many of the pills prescribed to me that I soon fell into unconsciousness. I awoke two-

-and-a-half days later with blood all over the place; the shame that I now felt was immense. But more importantly I now realized that a miracle had taken place – I

was alive. I didn't know how or why, but felt that something greater and more powerful than me was keeping me on this earth. I took time to reflect upon the

suicide attempts and how it went against everything that I believed in – my core belief that we can overcome any and all obstacles in life. I looked hard at the

losses and the deep hurts in my life and recognized them to be significant and it was okay to acknowledge that, but I really didn't want to die anymore. Now I

really paid more attention to the reports and studies of some of the psychiatric drugs that could cause suicidal ideation. I slowly started the process of weaning

myself off of the drugs because I still felt such despair but I realized the meds were not helping me with these feelings and thoughts; they only kept me numb,

confused and concerned with the side effects. I am mindful that some medications are of immense help for others struggling with mental health challenges, but for

me they were toxic.

I do know the losses in my life and some of the trauma and abuse I have experienced can cause one to become suicidal but I also feel quite strongly that the over-

prescribing of psychiatric drugs and the shunning I experienced from so many helped me to go down that dark road of suicide. To this day I can still feel and think

thoughts of suicide when overcome by sadness over the loss of my children, friends and lost hopes and dreams of my life. But my mind is clearer now. I am drug

free and I have found a new support system of caring and loving friends who don't push me away when I am feeling overwhelmed by life. That peer support has

made all the difference. I also eat right, exercise, meditate, and take time to relax and express my creativity – whether it is performing music on guitar, singing, playing the drums, gardening, cooking, writing, observing nature, or listening to music. Advocating for others has also helped me to heal. Sharing openly about

suicide is a powerful way for me to help others who have been so hurt in life that suicide seems like the only viable option. It is not – we must overcome our fears

and prejudices around the issues of suicide and learn to listen and embrace those who are suffering in life – we need to end 'The Silence of Suicide'.

DEFENDING SUICIDE

In defense of suicide

29

Kathryn Rosenfeld

Whether by religion, by politics, by secular ethics or human emotion, suicide is usually and still judged to be wrong or evil. This judgment reflects the tendency of power to exert control over individual lives, to erase individual agency and even the very notion that such agency can or should exist. It also reflects the common belief that one has the right to control the decisions and actions of another, even decisions as profoundly intimate as whether to go on living, based on one's own desires.

As an anarchist and a depressive, I can think of numerous situations in which suicide might be an acceptable, defensible, even a moral course of action.

My own suicide attempts have been undertaken for reasons both sound and dubious. When, at 15, I stole my mother's Valium and kept it under my pillow while I contemplated swallowing the whole bottle, I was hoping to be caught. I was enacting the proverbial cry for help, directed at upper-middle-class parents who disdained any and all expression of emotion, who seemed to view my adolescent pain chiefly as a ploy to distract them from their lucrative careers and busy high-society lives. That time, it worked: my mother providentially went looking for her sleeping pills that very night. I was in bed with the lights out when she came into my room. She sat down on the floor next to my low bed, arms around her knees, a move so uncharacteristic that it made me understand she was genuinely upset. Seeming small and oddly, imperfectly human on the carpet in her nightgown, she asked me why I had done it. Did I really believe I had to resort to such an act of piracy in order to get her attention?

169

Later that year and the next, when I sat on my bed and squeezed a scarf tightly around my neck, or pressed a razor blade into my wrist, I was hoping *no one* would walk in. My goal then was not to be caught, but truly to release myself from overwhelming pain. I was dealing with major depression from within the powerlessness of adolescence, I felt utterly unlovable, and my parents seemed incapable of understanding or caring. My mother thought it best not to indulge my solipsism, while my father was incensed at my inability to keep my grades up. When I complained that I didn't feel motivated – language I knew then to describe the state I now understand as depression – he exploded, 'You'd better *get* motivated!' One night as he quizzed me for a history exam, I tried to stay focused on the study questions while systematically slicing up the friendship bracelet tied around my wrist, using the same razor blade with which, the day before, I'd made the cut that the bracelet now concealed. When my father noticed what I was doing, he snapped at me to cut it out and get back to work.

My motivation was essentially the same when, at 27, I sat at my desk, once again holding a blade to my wrist. My girlfriend had dumped me for the second time, I was living alone in a new city, and I felt myself spiraling uncontrollably downward into a lightless singularity from which I would never emerge. That time, it was my cat who saved me. She walked into the room and somehow knew what was happening, saw that I was not within myself, and immediately began to issue a raw, alarmed meow that I had never heard before. It was enough to snap me out of my self-obliterating trance. Those other, teenage attempts had ended when I drew blood or began to black out, and found that, entirely counter to my desperate desire, I couldn't go through with it.

In trying to explain these failed attempts, I often find myself thinking of Jeff Goldblum's foreboding line from *Jurassic Park*: 'Life finds a way.' Or, what songwriter Ysaye Barnwell called 'life's longing for itself'. What Freud called Eros, the Life Drive.

Despite what we may long for and attempt to effect – what we may truly feel to be the best, or only, course of action – implacable Life resists us like a magnet. We may, in our human hubris, believe we can safely rebirth dinosaurs into the world, but *life finds a way*.

That last suicide attempt scared me enough – I'd thought that, having survived my teenage years, I would never end up back there – that within a month I was on antidepressants. The meds seem to keep me from sliding over that threshold into action. Yet suicide remains a foundational part of me. Nowadays suicide feels almost like an old friend, calming in her familiarity. We've been together so long that I know how to read her moods, how to tell the difference between slipping with relief into her murky oasis, and scrounging frantically for pills or blades or whatever else might do the job. The latter has come to seem the less attractive option: too much worry, too much work. But that other mood of suicide, in which it expands beyond an act into a state of mind, is a place of psychic respite to which I return often. When anxiety and depression become too overwhelming, when I have no more energy to give to the struggle of living, as we anarchists and madfolk do, without filters, with nerves raw and exposed to all the world's misery and cruelty, when all my efforts seem to be momentary puffs of smoke against the tendency of things to suck – then, I can retreat into the fantasy of what it would be like not to live. In this way, suicide has my back: a visit to its soothing shadows can be the open pressure valve that allows me to go on living.

Huey P. Newton, cofounder of the Black Panthers, titled his 1973 memoir *Revolutionary Suicide*. He called this 'the way of liberation' and contrasted it with 'reactionary suicide', the ultimate response to life under murderous poverty and soul-destroying oppression. The liberatory form of suicide, on the other hand, is actually self-defense in the face of overwhelming odds: not the symbolic act of martyrdom that some revolutionaries dream of, but rather a decision to fight back against a system that kills you slowly, knowing that your resistance will probably get you killed quickly. 'It is better', Newton wrote, 'to oppose the forces that would drive me to self-murder than to endure them.' As an absolute refusal to accept life under unlivable conditions, revolutionary suicide is an excellent example of the Life Drive in action.

But the connection between revolution and suicide is an old one, which Newton tried to reimagine in a proactive light. The history of revolution is peppered with the suicide of revolutionaries, and the despair that comes of fighting all one's life against a seemingly immutable, insurmountable enemy is only one reason.

On November 10, 1887, five men sat in prison in Chicago, waiting to be hanged for being anarchists. (They'd been convicted as accessories to the murder of a policeman in the infamous Haymarket Riot the previous year, even though most were not present at the event, and none could be linked evidentially to the implicated bomb, which most historians now agree was thrown by a police-planted provocateur.) But on November 11, only four men went to the gallows: Louis Lingg, reputedly the most 'hot-headed' of the bunch, had killed himself in his cell the night before, with a smuggled-in dynamite plug that he put in his mouth and lit like a cigar. His last revolutionary act was to deny the state the ability to take his life.

On November 3, 2006, Chicago musician and antiwar activist Malachi Ritscher set himself on fire on the shoulder of the Kennedy Expressway during morning rush hour, as a protest against the US war on Iraq. In his revolutionary suicide-by-fire, Ritscher was in illustrious historical company: the Buddhist monks who famously engaged in public self-immolation during the Vietnam War come to mind as an obvious example. Some people who knew Ritscher revealed (and he himself admitted, in his suicide note) that he'd been depressed and struggling with alcoholism, as though this information negated his political intentions, when in fact it was exactly the point. Ritscher was one of us 'sensitive types', often called radicals or crazies, who could no longer stand to live in a world full of hypocrisy and murderous domination. In resolving to remove himself from this world, he resolved that his death should be impactful. He wrote, 'Many people will think that I should not be able to choose the time and manner of my own death. My position is that I only get one death, I want it to be a good one ... if I am required to pay for your barbaric war, I choose not to live in your world.'

On February 20, 2005, writer Hunter S. Thompson shot himself in the head at his home in rural Colorado. Like the rest of his legions of fans, I was at first shocked by his suicide. But as soon as I learned more about the circumstances, I got over any temptation to romanticize his death as some blaze-of-glory finale to his Gonzo life. The notion is equally absurd that blowing one's head off is what comes of a lifetime of drugs and oppositionality. In fact, by the time he died Thompson had suffered years of constant pain due to a hip replacement and multiple other ailments. Many of those closest to him said publicly that his suicide had not come as a surprise – that he'd said all along he would end his life when he became a burden to himself and others. Nonetheless, in the 2008 documentary *Gonzo: The Life and Work of Hunter S. Thompson*, the writer's ex-wife expressed that she felt his death had been a cop-out, because the world needed his voice now more than ever. All I could think as I watched the film was, it's a good thing they divorced, as she must not have loved him, or must have loved the legend more than the real person – or why would she want him to go on suffering?

On April 19, 2006, my mother died at the age of 61, in the intensive care unit of Sloan–Kettering Hospital in New York, where she'd lain in an induced coma for several weeks. At that point it had been five or six months since she'd been outside. The treatment for her leukemia– her second bout in eight years – involved her confinement to a hospital room, which no one was allowed to enter without donning scrubs and masks. When, sometime in March, I arrived sweating from my bike ride to the hospital, she exclaimed with her usual motherly alarm that I must be freezing without a jacket. My father just laughed. 'It's turned into spring while you've been shut up in here,' he quipped in jovial tones.

Throughout the period of my mother's dying, we never spoke of her approaching end; we contorted ourselves into impressive knots of feigned optimism. Even when, to Mom's visible relief, the decision was made to induce a coma, we said that she was 'going to sleep so that she could get better'. Our family culture of denial prohibited any mention of the obvious – even after Mom was actually dead.

My mother was a consummate rationalist. She had no time for the sentimental hysterics of religion, especially when it came to subjects like death. She vehemently supported reproductive freedom and the right to die. She did not consider old age a necessarily desirable goal. She often said that she did not fear death, only suffering.

So why, then, did she end up dying in an ICU (intensive care unit) cell, her body riddled with machine tubes and toxic chemicals, having lived her final months deprived of fresh air and free movement? Did she have a change of heart, and conclude that the chance for a few more years of life was worth the risk of living her last days in a hospital, unable to touch or see the faces of her loved ones? Did she relinquish herself to some sort of faith, which suddenly revealed itself after a lifetime of skepticism? Or, was she motivated by a sense of obligation to my father and, perhaps, to my sister and me? Did looking death in the face lead a woman who'd always taken her own council to place the perceived desires of others above the ability to control the circumstances of her own death? I will never know the answers to these questions. But I do know that if and when I become terminally ill, I'll go to just about any length to die in a manner and context of my own choosing.

I can't figure out what all the fuss is about human life anyway. There are way, way too many of us, and this, along with the conditions of industrial civilization, make life at best a ceaseless struggle, and at worst a living hell for most of us. To bring another human into this mess strikes me as the ultimate act of selfish cruelty, and, if you have access to the means to prevent it, unforgivable. My anti-natalist position leads me to harbor a marked sympathy for the tenets of the Church of Euthanasia – absent my distaste for religion, I'd probably join. According to their FAQs, my choice not to breed means I'm already a member anyhow. The Church of Euthanasia's slogan is 'Save the Planet – Kill Yourself'. Its One Commandment is 'Thou shall not procreate', and its Four Pillars are suicide, abortion, cannibalism, and sodomy. The C of E's mission is to educate the public about these and all other '*voluntary* forms of population reduction'.

What particularly attracts me about this, aside from the part about how we all need to stop having babies, is its utter reversal of the sanctity of human life as professed by most religions. Suicide isn't a sin – in fact it may be a way of doing right by the planet. There's nothing holy about the fact that your father's sperm found your mother's egg and nine months later your mother squeezed you out. Your existence here on earth could not be less significant. Some people find this thought profoundly threatening, but to me it is a great comfort.

Ultimately, what has kept me from offing myself is other people. While suicide might in some circumstances be understandable, moral, even self-caring, it is not kind to others. I've known people who've had a loved one commit suicide, and it fucks you up in unique ways. If I ever start down that road again, my progress must be blocked by the question of whether I could stand to do that to the people I love. And if I ever find even this obstacle unequal to the pain of living, I'll at least figure out a way to take something deserving with me when I go.

Addendum

A couple of months after this chapter was written, a beloved friend took their own life by hanging. It happened at their parents' house, where they'd been staying, isolated from friends and community, telling those who tried to reach out not to worry, that they were fine, while progressively withdrawing into depression. They were in their early 20s, brilliant, beautiful, vibrant, all heart, loved by a vast network of friends both close and casual. An energizing light of the radical and queer communities in Chicago and beyond. And yet they chose to die.

For the still-living it is difficult to understand why someone apparently with so much going for them would make such a choice. Anger is understandable and, as a part of grief, inevitable.

Our friend, like so many of us out here on the fringes, was tortured by mental illness. For me to blame a comrade in madness for choosing suicide would be hypocritical at best. I've been to that edge myself so many times. I'm all too familiar with that threshold past which the pain of existence screams louder than all the voices begging you to live, where the darkness at the bottom of yourself blots out even the love of others. But yes, I am angry – at this horrible, hateful world we've created that makes merely staying alive a daily struggle, especially if you're not straight, white, or rich. Some say this is a cop-out, that the suicide gives in to weakness or takes the easy way out. Bullshit. This world kills us all, slowly or otherwise. Sometimes just surviving can be an act of resistance, but sometimes, like any struggle against overwhelming odds, it becomes too much. Those who choose their own death while they still can are heroes, in a way. Their lives and deaths remind us to keep fighting and keep living, for each other.

A red sadness: My dad's story

30

Chrissie Hinde

My dad committed suicide when I was 8. The harsh reality of this didn't strike home at first. I remember reacting in a matter of fact way, thinking 'Oh that makes my mum a widow'. My parents were separated at the time and I hadn't seen my dad since I was 5.

I was about 12 when the full weight of my dad's suicide struck home to me. I started having recurrent nightmares in which I was being chased by a huge house filled with writhing snakes that was trying to flatten me. I struggled to get to sleep at night because I was scared I wouldn't wake up. I think my dad's suicide brought the reality of death to my consciousness for the first time. I remember wondering why people made such a big deal of Jesus' death when he had the good fortune to come back to life. I'd not taken in the reality of his torture, betrayal and abandonment before he died, so it seemed to my 12-year-old mind that he got off lightly.

After my mum had given me and my siblings the news of Dad's suicide I don't remember us ever talking about it again. It was only much later as an adult that I had the courage to ask my mum more about my dad. I didn't go to my dad's funeral. My dad's family was upset and angry with my mum for not staying with my dad so I guess she didn't want to take us kids into a hostile atmosphere.

I wish I had a supportive atmosphere in which to talk about my dad as a young teenager. I think this would have really helped me. My early teens were one of the most painful and difficult times in my life. I felt very low and lacking in confidence. I became very shy and would spend long periods of time alone in my room. I thought I was ugly and that no one would ever love me. My mum did take me for psychotherapy, but it didn't help much. I was expected to talk about painful things when what I think I needed was more structured guidance and loving support. My mum did her best, but she was working very long hours and was also struggling with her own depression. She had also had no support over my dad's death.

Part of what helped me come out of this tough phase was getting my first boyfriend who made me feel attractive and desirable; another significant part was joining an evangelical church in which I had a strong sense of family and belonging, and being wanted. I later moved on from this kind of church because I couldn't agree that there was only one valid faith and didn't like feeling forced into a set of beliefs. I do feel very grateful for the role the church played in my life. I now find myself at home with my Quaker and Buddhist practice, which helps keep me sane and grounded.

My life since has been and continues to be deeply affected by my dad's death. It's such a great privilege to be able to write for this book because I've longed to tell this story, and flesh out the details for a long time. It has also brought fresh pain and deep sadness, as each time I delve more deeply into my past and learn more about my dad's story there are new insights which can be loaded with grief. I've talked about my dad's death in numerous therapy sessions over the years, but to be able to tell the full story feels like a really important next step, and something I can share.

Last year I attended a 'Suicidal Wisdom' workshop in which we used creative methods to explore the suicide of loved ones. It was wonderful to be with others in the same boat. I'd never had this experience before and felt deeply moved by it. I also loved the workshop title because it was acknowledging that suicide may be a wise and desirable choice in certain circumstances. It doesn't have to be a tragedy for the one who dies; it could be a welcome release from unbearable or relentless suffering.

After the 'Suicidal Wisdom' workshop I offered to lead a workshop at a gestalt conference in which we would tell our 'suicide stories'. It's so healing to be able to talk openly about this great taboo, particularly with others who share suicide experiences. The workshop was the best attended in the conference. I was really heartened by the number of people who, like me, seemed really keen to share their stories.

One participant shared how he made a serious suicide attempt, lost consciousness and then survived. He said the experience of almost dying had been a blissful release and it was really hard to find himself still alive. He had a struggle to come to terms with this. I was very moved by him, because it was like having my dad in the room. There were many similarities between this man and my dad, as he also had children and was separated from his family when he attempted suicide. He said he'd got to the point where life was so grim and desolate that having children was no longer an impediment to suicide. And I understood what he meant. I felt very close to him. It was great not to have to feel responsible for him. I didn't have to worry that, because he'd done it before, he'd be more likely to do it again. We could just meet as two human beings sharing our story. As a mental health professional I feel duty bound to have a risk assessment checklist in my head, yet the best conversations happen when we don't have an agenda.

My dad was diagnosed with schizophrenia and I remember my mum saying that a mental illness was far worse than a physical one. My dad's life was made all the grimmer I believe by the archaic and unenlightened psychiatric services of the day. I often wonder if he had had the help of community mental health services that we have today with a shift towards a recovery culture, whether he would have survived. My uncle said he used to complain about his medication making him a zombie. My cousin told me of a time when they visited my dad in hospital and he talked of feeling demeaned by activities like making baskets and paper hats, and being told he was rebellious for growing a beard.

I hate the thought of my dad incarcerated in those desolate old psychiatric wards of the large asylums. I found a letter in which he described hospital as like prison. I remember once when we visited him, he stole my mum's car keys and escaped. I remember another time when they came to section him. I think it was early morning and as a 5-year-old all I could make sense of was that people were taking my dad away and he was protesting.

I found out very recently from my dad's brother and sister that my dad had scarlet fever when he was 2 years old and spent weeks in isolation in hospital without visits from family. This must have been really traumatic for him and probably made his psychiatric admissions later in his life feel all the more distressing because of his early childhood hospital incarceration.

I gravitated towards working in mental health I think, as a way of understanding my dad's experience and protecting myself against the danger of my own madness by immersing myself in knowledge and experience of mental health. I think I also wanted to help others who'd had a similar experience to my dad because I wasn't able to help my dad. I qualified as an occupational therapist and then went on to do gestalt psychotherapy training because I wanted to go deeper into what makes us tick as humans, and what makes things go wrong.

I think I've been very lucky to have had the life I've had so far. At the Suicidal Wisdom workshop we did a two-chair exercise where you switch roles to 'get into the shoes of the other', by shifting chairs. I switched roles with 'my dad' and what came up for me playing the part of my dad was: 'I'm dying so you can live your life to the full. I will no longer be holding you back.' It's impossible to really know if that's what my dad thought but I think he did have a big sense of failure and abandonment. I also think he'd lost hope and sense of purpose for his own life.

My dad's suicide felt like a very deliberate act. He had been living with his mum and dad in Lancaster. He travelled down to London and threw himself off London Bridge into the Thames. He left his clothes neatly folded by the side of the bridge. It took three days before his body was found and he was unrecognisable but for a scar on his forehead that he'd had since childhood. My uncle said having to identify the body was a terrible experience.

Ironically I spent some time in my early twenties living very close to London Bridge. By chance a colleague of mine offered me a room in her flat in Bermondsey. I used to cross over London Bridge countless times on route into town and I always thought about my dad.

I've made a point of trying to fill in the gaps in information about my dad mainly through talking to my mum and my cousin and more recently my siblings and members of Dad's family. It's been like putting together a jigsaw with a sense of urgency to have a more complete picture. We all have our own versions made up from a patchwork of facts and imaginings, and they don't all fit together neatly.

My dad's parents were working class with very little money. My granddad (Dad's dad) fought in the First World War and was discharged on mental health grounds. I don't think he ever recovered from the trauma of that war. He didn't work and was very childlike. You couldn't have a deep conversation with him, but he liked to tell stories and play the piano very loudly. It was as if he coped with the trauma of his war experiences by completely cutting himself off from them and that somehow the trauma passed on to the next generation. My dad was one of four siblings and only his eldest brother escaped having any mental health problems. I realise this is just my theory but it makes sense to me.

My grandma (Dad's mum) was bright and dynamic, a real powerhouse. She used to clean people's houses. She carried on doing it into her eighties when she described herself as cleaning for the old people. My dad was bright and hardworking and came to represent all that she hadn't had for herself. She used her hard-earned money to send my dad to a private school.

He excelled at school and got a scholarship to go to Cambridge. This was like my grandma's dream come true, but it must have put my dad under tremendous pressure to live up to all she dreamed of for him.

My dad must have had a strong dose of imposter syndrome as a working-class northern lad in those lofty corridors of Cambridge. Apparently they laughed at his suitcase and he couldn't fathom the excessive cutlery in the dining room. He had his first psychotic break-down there but did recover sufficiently to scrape through with a 3rd-class degree. My cousin also has a theory that my dad's illness was brought on by being asked to study Russian during his National Service in the RAF prior to starting at Cambridge. The Russian was meant to prime him for spying on the Russians by translating Russian military radio communications.

My parents got married in their early twenties and they both got jobs as teachers. My mum describes the first two years of their marriage as blissful. I think they were very in love. But my dad started withdrawing and probably found it really hard when us kids came along. I think it was mainly my mum's choice to have children. First my sister, then two foster brothers aged 2 and 4 years, then me. They went from zero to four kids in two years. My dad found sanctuary by retreating to his study where my brother said he would smoke and drink coffee into the night. During this time my dad got an MA in French, whilst my mum felt like she was living as a single parent.

We went to live in Kenya when I was 3, to fulfil my mum's dream to go to Africa. My dad got a job at a teacher training college. Mum said my dad was very happy there at first and they settled in well with my dad playing a more active role in the family. But then he had a big breakdown after two years in Kenya and ended up in hospital. This was shortly followed by my parents separating. My mum felt that she couldn't look after us kids and my dad and she had to make a choice. If my mum had had a loving upbringing and support from her family and friends when my dad withdrew or was unwell then maybe my dad would still be alive today. But my mum didn't have those things and she didn't have professional support to cope with my dad, and I can't blame her for giving up. I also don't want to minimise the stress of being with a partner who can become very psychotic. It's very possible that in my mum's shoes I would have made the same decision.

My uncle, Dad's brother, gave me a parcel of my dad's letters and notes a few years ago. I found a poem by my dad which he'd written after he separated from my mum and was back in England: '… but of this you can be sure | There's nothing in this life that love cannot cure |

Maybe we'll kiss again with a love that's true | Maybe we'll share again a life anew.' I do think it's tragic that my parents' marriage which was initially filled with such hope and promise, ended with such disillusionment and torment.

When my parents separated, my dad returned to his parents' home in Lancaster two days after his 35th birthday in 1968. It cuts me up to think of my dad making that lonely journey back to England, leaving us behind, not knowing when he'd see us again. My mum told my dad if he got a job and a house we'd come back to him, but that never happened. When my dad returned to England he did succeed in getting a job but I think it proved too stressful for him and he was in and out of hospital. We stayed in Kenya for another three years and then returned to England ... My dad committed suicide on 10th July 1971. It was the same year we returned to England.

I think my dad chose my mum because she was in many ways like his own mother: strong and ambitious. I don't think he ever had the experience of feeling that he was fine just as he was; he had to keep striving to prove himself. If I could time-travel back to those dark months leading up to my dad's death I'd like to say to him: 'Just enjoy the roses in the garden, and watching the seagulls at Morecambe Bay, and listening to Beethoven and immersing yourself in mathematical equations and infinity because these things are the essence of life. You are not a failure, you are good enough just as you are.'

With Dad's notes was an application form he'd completed three years before he died. In it he describes all his many achievements. He must have had some hope at that stage in late 1968, but then his hope must have run out. I find that very sad to think about.

My dad seems like a great guy in so many ways. People describe him as gentle, sensitive, intellectual and deep with something to fulfil. He loved classical music, particularly Beethoven, Chopin and Tchaikovsky. He loved maths. He studied languages: French, German and Russian, Esperanto and Swahili. He used to play rugby at school and liked cycling and swimming. He played the piano for hours. He was very religious and my grandma said he was always praying. I guess he had a lot to pray for in his last years. I found a kind a prayer amongst my dad's notes:

> *O vision ineffable, what majesty sublime,*
> *To shape my soul more capable*
> *And make me want to climb*
> *To the top of highest mountains and sing your praises*
> *But worldly tasks await me here below*

And though I often fail I know your love will prevail
To see me to the end.
(Inspired by watching seagulls on Morecambe beach – end of 1968)

Some of Dad's notes were written in French, so recently I decided to try translating them using Google. It was a very moving experience to type these words in, which were written all those years ago and see the English translation pop up word by word:

Ton ame est immortelle et les pleurs vont tarir
Your soul is immortal and the tears will dry up

Je suis rouge d'une tristesse aupres de laquelle la nuit la plus
sombre est une lumiere eblouissante
I am a red sadness with which the darkest night is a dazzling light

Il voyait un ocean sans bonnes
He saw an ocean without good

I hate the thought of my dad taking himself on his last journey alone, no one knowing of his intentions, dying alone. I'd like a different kind of life and death for him, surrounded by his family. Yet I'm sure when he passed from this life he will have felt relief that all his torment and unfulfilled hopes and dreams were over. Maybe for him this was a sane and courageous act in the face of relentless hospital admissions, loss of contact with loved ones and the prospect of endless days of half living, doped up on medication, or constantly failing and relapsing. Maybe it was his way of saying, 'This isn't good enough and this not-enoughness is too much to bear!' I would hate to ever take that choice away from anyone.

Learning/discussion points:

- I think it would have been really helpful to be able to talk about my dad's suicide when I was a child and to have someone help make sense of it with me.

- I think having community support from mental health services for both my mum and dad would have really helped, especially if it wasn't just focused on taking medication.

- Telling my story has been a very healing experience for me, and helping to create a culture where it's OK to talk openly about suicide.

31

An epilogue:
Suicide and sense-making

Alec Grant

My encounters with suicide

To the best of my recollection, I've had six significant encounters with suicide in my 61 years of being alive. The first was when I was 17, in the British Royal Air Force (RAF). An airman I barely knew, slightly older than me, hanged himself from the top of some kind of navigation or radio tower. In the obituary section of the *RAF News* a little later, he was described as having 'died suddenly'. Although shaken by his death I remember thinking this obituary funny and ironic at the time. Now I know that its wording reflected a broad cultural tendency to sanitise narratives of death by suicide. It was the late 1960s after all.

Encounter two happened in 1974 when my mother hanged herself. She tied a rope to one of the bedroom doors of the council house where she lived with my father, put the noose around her neck and threw herself over the banister of the staircase leading to the ground floor. She measured the rope fairly precisely, so that she landed with her feet 12 inches from the floor and her body facing, and a yard away from, the front door of the house. She was found by my father as he came home from work a few hours later. Subsequently, the stories on the street and in the clinic were that she wanted to punish. Opinions varied as to who exactly the intended recipient/s of this might be.

Encounter three happened during my first psychotherapy training in the early to mid-1980s. On the 1st of March 1983, the novelist and journalist Arthur Koestler and his wife Cynthia committed suicide using a combination of barbiturates and alcohol, he because of terminal illnesses, she because she did not wish to go on living without him. Both left suicide notes, stating the above as rational grounds for what they did together. It seemed to me then that this was quite reasonable in the circumstances and I remember having a heated debate with a mental health researcher who insisted that both of them must have been, de facto and by default, mentally ill.

His insistence reflected the official psychiatric story informing mental health professional and lay reactions at the time. One of the effects of this durable narrative, for it persists, is to sanction a kind of dismissive closure on suicide – framing it as an issue not worthy of too much exploration or curiosity. This serves a cultural function of course, around the need to avoid the bogeyman of ultimate self-harm, the fearful dark side of what it might mean to be fully human. (When speaking with my colleagues in healthcare higher education about the project of this book as it developed, some screwed up their faces in disgust, while others tried to trivialise it by making a joke of it: 'Nice bedtime reading, then?' was a frequent comment. This signals to me a one-dimensional investment in life and healthcare: physical and material waste is OK to talk about, proceduralise and process, but a sustained and detailed focus on wasting lives is verboten.)

Encounter four was when I had the privilege, two decades later, to co-supervise Ian Marsh's PhD: *Suicide: Foucault, history and truth*, subsequently published by Cambridge University Press (Marsh, 2010). His original and provocative thesis critically examined the historical and cultural forces influencing contemporary approaches to understanding suicide as a public health problem. Drawing on Foucauldian theory, Marsh told a story of how suicide has come to be seen primarily as a psychiatric issue through processes of social construction. His work challenged the assumptions and certainties embedded in societal master narratives (to be given further mention below) concerning suicide and the suicidal.

Encounters number five and six were when I tried to take my own life on two separate occasions in my mid-fifties. I have spent the last few years trying to make contextual and existential sense of these last two encounters in different ways, including writing (e.g., Grant, 2011b). Like many of the contributors in this book, I have found this helpful in progressing my life.

Master narratives and storying lives

The urge to account always seems to follow the intention to commit suicide, failed suicide attempts, or being left to pick up the pieces of someone else's suicide. We need to make sense of these issues and events, extract meaning from them, attribute blame and innocence, lay things to rest, move on to the next chapter of our lives.

This is not surprising if we accept the general premise of storied lives. Various scholars in the social and human sciences, and in linguistics and the humanities, have long argued for the idea of life as story, sometimes called narrative. The general idea is that we shape our lives, in terms of meaning, action, and that which we take for granted, by the spoken or written conversations we have with ourselves and with others. In order to do this, we necessarily have to draw on a stock of stories and vocabularies that pre-date us historically and/or exist in a state of authority, respectability, or 'just so-ness'. These big stories are sometimes called 'master narratives', 'grand narratives', 'discourses', 'cultural narratives' or 'implicit narratives', and are a ready source of off-the-peg wisdom.

Such a view is complemented in contemporary literature. In *The Sense of an Ending*, for example, Julian Barnes uses a livestock confinement metaphor to describe life:

> *In those days, we imagined ourselves as being kept in some kind of holding pen, waiting to be released into our lives. ... How were we to know that our lives had in any case begun, that some advantage had already been gained, some damage already inflicted? Also, that our release would only be into a larger holding pen, whose boundaries would be at first indiscernible.* (Barnes, 2011, p. 10)

The metaphor of the holding pen helps us conceptualise important aspects of the big stories that we are always, inevitably, caught up in, and their pros and cons. Master narratives (holding pens) contain us in socially accepted accounts of how life is and should be and create boundaries for us. They give many of us an illusion of the world complete and provide a correspondingly delimited language to describe it. All of this can confer benefits and security to some, a sense of right and wrong, good and bad. Conversely, this state of affairs can stifle and frustrate others, triggering their need to think about, describe and act on the world differently, using different grammars, different words, different concepts.

Storying suicide: Metaphors and suicide notes

There doesn't seem to be much of a developed language, language stock, or big story to make positive sense or meaning of suicide, and this shouldn't be surprising. Thus, in 'suicide as pathology' stories, the grammar of suicide is often unavoidably negative and pejorative, described in terms of a lack, or an absence, or moral transgression in relation to un-reason, indecency, cowardice, blame, selfishness. Strong emotional reactions such as grief and anger fire this grammar, but these are arguably connected to the tacitly held and indiscernible cultural assumptions around the need to toe the line, play the game, abide by the rules, stay in the pen.

More specifically, there are material artefacts that both contribute to storying suicide and constitute stories or sub-stories in their own right. What is the status of the suicide note in this regard? We are all held to account for our lives on a daily basis, without it being too much of a problem most of the time. Kafka (1925/1953) explores this vividly in his novel *The Trial*. The central character in the story is a bank official, Joseph K., who is informed that he is on trial for a crime that is not stated. He is allowed complete freedom of movement to go about his business during the protracted duration of the trial proceedings, which are extremely informal and unspecified. He seeks understanding of what it is he's accused of, but finds none, only that his pressing need for clarity is regarded as further evidence of his guilt.

The suicide note may be regarded as an attempt to seek such clarity, or bequeath understanding. Or it may sometimes signify an act of contrition, or a purchase ticket for forgiveness and closure – a kind of moral token of exchange in the narrative economy of life and death. The Koestler notes emerged from the 1980s as artefacts of social history. In all of these instances, the suicide note arguably belongs simultaneously to everyone and no one.

And to what extent does it contribute to metaphorical understandings of the relational significance of the suicide event, as in, for example, 'he wrote his final testimony', or 'she gave a good account of herself'. Lakoff and Johnson (2003) help us understand how metaphors structure our understanding of experiences of relations with others and life generally through narrative. The chapters in *Our Encounters with Suicide* are replete with telling examples, including the following: 'life sucks' (does life outside me suck, or does it suck the life out of me?); 'cracking hearts' (you have broken my heart, or my heart broke itself); 'swinging the lead' (we don't believe you; I can't believe that you don't believe me); 'emotionally skinned' (my emotions have been cut from me; others have done this); 'walking through darkness' (I can't find the switch for light or clarity in my life; the lights have been switched off by others, life, circumstances); 'suicide as the ultimate coping strategy' (anticipating the need for a new kind of self-help book, an inverse of the Samuel Smiles variety); 'battling with suicide' (keeping suicide at bay in a kind of siege; the lone individual surrounded by an army of life-sucking demons).

Metaphors such as these may be the best available 'off the shelf' options to confer meaning on suicide or symbolise the celebration of continued living. They serve to story anger, grief and atonement. But what kind of metaphors might be employed to simply justify suicide as a reasonable and moral choice in the context of an unbearable existence – an issue that's appeared several times in this book? There are examples in its pages of political and medical metaphors, representing a need to exit from life angrily. Will there ever be a time when it is culturally acceptable for people to say goodbye to life calmly, with minimal raging against the dying of the light, and with no payoff either in terms of rancour left behind or hopes of '… a de-personalised after-life beyond due confines of space, time and matter and beyond the limits of our comprehension' (Arthur Koestler, Wikipedia)?

Sanitised accounts and suicide experts

One thing's for sure: all of the chapters in this book are testimony to the struggles of contributing authors with living and dying. All are attempts at sense-making around suicide and, in spite of the inevitability of shared concepts, all convey unique stories told by 'experts by experience'. All give the lie to sanitised accounts that implicitly claim to neatly 'wrap up' the suicide phenomenon. This is because the more such accounts try to pretend that they are not just one more big story or master narrative in a succession of master narratives, the more they are doomed to fail, as :

> … *suicide, as a discursively constituted phenomenon, will always resist complete description, if for no other reason than as a cultural product it lacks any unchanging essence that could act as a stabilising centre by which to secure such a centre.* (Marsh, 2010, pp. 6–7)

Appendix 1
Maytree: A sanctuary for the suicidal

Maytree: Meeting the need for non-medical short-term residential care for those in suicidal crisis

Maytree was founded in 2002 by Paddy Bazeley and Michael Knight. Both came from a background with Samaritans where they realised that for many people the help lines and drop-in centres of the voluntary sector were not enough, and yet often suicidal people did not want or feel ready to access longer-term medical psychiatric support, through fear of stigma or hospitalisation.

We offer a brief stay of five days in a non-medical setting with space and time to be listened to, heard and to reflect, in the hope that the belief that life is worth living will be restored. This time period has been chosen as it is short enough for guests experiencing a suicidal crisis not to become dependent, but long enough to be potentially transformational and for people to make the decision that they want to live.

We know we see some of those most hard to reach. Approximately half our guests have not had recent contact with mental health services, 70% have tried to kill themselves once, and 17% three or more times. Our guests pay nothing for their stay.

Maytree's aims and objectives

- To support people through a suicidal crisis.
- To provide a safe place and a turning point for people with suicidal thoughts.

The target outcomes

- Guests experience a significant decrease in their suicide risk.
- Family and friends of guests have significantly reduced risk of bereavement by suicide.
- People with suicidal thoughts or their family and friends have improved mental well-being following phone or email support.

Project activities and outputs

- Those affected by suicidal thoughts are made aware of Maytree's support through a strong online presence and by networking with other organisations working with people with mental health issues such as GPs, hospitals, psychotherapists and community groups. Our guests come from all over the UK.
- Phone and email-based support are provided to at least 800 people with suicidal thoughts or friends or family members over the course of a year. Where appropriate, callers and emailers are cross-referred to organisations able to help them address their specific worries.
- Those in the midst of a suicidal crisis will be provided with the opportunity to stay in the non-medical, peaceful and homely environment at Maytree, which can hold four 'guests' at a time, a practical monthly optimum of 16 guests. The service runs 24 hours a day, 365 days a year, including over Christmas.
- Carefully selected and trained volunteers and staff spend time with the guests over their 5-day, 4-night stay, giving them an opportunity to discuss their troubles without fear of judgement.
- Guests are given a goodbye letter when they leave. This is intended to consolidate the benefits of the stay. It will typically state the

underlying core pain that has brought them to Maytree, any increase in self-awareness and the rediscovery of (often forgotten) strengths. The goodbye letter acts as a physical reminder of their stay and the intense, often life-changing, experience.

- A guest cannot stay a second time, hence the stress on attempting a 'good ending' – the exact opposite of suicide. Throughout the stay considerable time is given to set up sources of ongoing support, linking guests up to relevant services.

Longer-term impact

A full evaluation in 2006 and follow-up research in 2009, completed by the Tavistock and Portman NHS Trust, were extremely positive about the longer-term impact of Maytree's work. They found a statistically significant reduction in distress levels from the clinical to the normal range among guests who stayed at Maytree over a 3-month period. Further, in follow-up interviews three to five months after their stay most guests had continued to improve and attributed this largely to the stay. The report concludes: *'Maytree makes a unique contribution to suicide prevention ... there is a clear need for more centres based on the Maytree model.'*

Maytree and its approach were also praised in Mind's recent inquiry into acute and crisis mental health care which states: *'We would like to see the defining concept of residential acute care shift from that of the medical ward towards that of a retreat; providing humane, respectful, personalised care in a comfortable environment.'*

Facts and figures

- Maytree has helped 6,300 people in suicidal crisis since opening and 850 people have stayed as guests. Last year we helped more than 800 people.

- For every completed suicide an average of six people are deeply affected or traumatised. Those with suicide in the family are at significantly higher risk of committing suicide themselves.

- It has been estimated that every suicide costs the national economy £1.29 million (Platt, S. et al, 2006, *Evaluation of the First Phase of 'Choose Life'*, Edinburgh: Scottish Executive Social Research). This includes direct costs (NHS treatment, emergency services, funerals), indirect costs (lost economic output whether paid, voluntary or caring) and of course the more intangible costs from grief and bereavement (lost output and treatment for bereavement and depression as a result of suicide).

- Maytree is therefore very cost effective – based on our own costs, every £1 invested in Maytree potentially saves the national economy up to £450.

- The time given to us by volunteers saves us £140,000 per year.

- Maytree's work is described as 'exemplary' by the Department of Health (DoH) and is cited in its *Consultation on Preventing Suicide in England*, published July 2011. Maytree was also given as an example of good practice in the DoH's *New Horizons* strategy.

These comments from our 2010/11 guest book provide an insight into the thoughts and feelings of our guests about the time they have spent at Maytree.

Maria's story

My time at Maytree was the most transformative period I have ever had, in terms of how I manage my depression. I have never experienced such warmth and such effective help – and it's so simple – just intensive talking therapy (with trained counsellors and with befrienders too) over five days. In a very normalising, 'home' type environment (house, own bedroom, big kitchen, free to do what you want).

I had such a sense of belonging and calm – and perversely enough I developed such a strong sense that I was perfectly 'normal' and not some crazy patient. Just a normal person who happened to be experiencing a terrible, terrible crisis, but one that could be talked through. We need more Maytrees. I truly believe that this place saves lives.

(Note: name changed for confidentiality reasons)

'Thank You' doesn't seem enough, but I want you to know that if I could do for others what you've all done for me, I'd be swinging from the rooftops.
I arrived a 'mess', falling apart, but I feel mentally stronger and better equipped to deal with my future.

My time has been filled with ups and downs but I have ultimately found the motivation and strength to start what is going to be the recovery that WILL get me on my feet and to love life once again!!

I doubt I'll ever find such a valuable place again, so I will always remember my stay here, the people that held my hand, and how it stopped me from falling over the edge.

Appendix 2
Useful links and contacts

Charity/ organisation	Contact details	Website	Details
Maytree	020 7263 70 70	www.maytree.org.uk	Maytree is a charity that offers a one-off four-night stay, in a calm and safe residential setting, to those at risk of suicide.
Samaritans	08457 90 90 90	www.samaritans.org	Contact Samaritans any time for confidential support.
Mind	0300 123 3393	www.mind.org.uk	Mind, the mental health charity. There to make sure anyone with a mental health problem has somewhere to turn for advice and support.
Young Minds	Parent helpline 0808 802 5544	www.youngminds.org.uk	Young Minds is the UK's leading charity committed to improving the emotional wellbeing and mental health of children and young people. Driven by their experiences they campaign, research and influence policy and practice.
CALM Campaign Against Living Miserably	Helpline 0800 58 58 58	www.thecalmzone.net	Our lines are open seven days a week, 5 p.m. to midnight. Calls are free from landlines, confidential, anonymous and they won't show up on your phone bill. Trained paid staff will be available to talk through problems, listen and offer information.
Rethink	Advice line 0300 5000 927	www.rethink.org	Rethink Mental Illness is a charity that believes a better life is possible for millions of people affected by mental illness.
Mental Health Foundation	Via their website	www.mentalhealth.org.uk	We are committed to reducing the suffering caused by mental ill health and to help everyone lead mentally healthier lives. We help people to survive, recover from and prevent mental health problems.

Editors and contributors

Editors

Fran Biley

The late Dr Francis C. Biley initially trained as a mental health and adult nurse and after holding a range of clinical and practice development posts moved into undergraduate and postgraduate research and teaching. He co-edited *Our Encounters with Madness* (PCCS Books, 2011) with Alec Grant and Hannah Walker. He was Associate Professor in the Centre for Qualitative Research at Bournemouth University, UK, Adjunct Professor of Nursing at Seton Hall University, New Jersey, USA, and a Governor of a local Foundation Trust hospital.

Alec Grant

Dr Alec Grant is a Principal Lecturer in the School of Nursing and Midwifery at the University of Brighton. He qualified as a mental health nurse in the mid-1970s and went on to study psychology, social science and psychotherapy. He is widely published in the fields of ethnography, autoethnography, clinical supervision, cognitive behavioural psychotherapy, and communication and interpersonal skills. For the last few years, his research interests have been in the area of narrative inquiry and writing, especially around mental health survival. He can be contacted by email at: A.Grant@brighton.ac.uk

Judith Haire

Judith was born in Kent. She left school at 15 and worked for an estate agent and a London advertising agency before going to college where she passed her A and S levels. After working for a further year she went to Sheffield University to read Political Theory and Institutions, graduating in 1981. She returned to work in advertising and went on to work in the civil service. At 37 her career was cut short when she experienced an acute psychotic episode. Once recovered she worked in the voluntary sector and studied at college. Judith has been published in *Mental Health Practice*, *Community Care*, and *Your Voice in Sheffield Mental Health* magazines, and her first book, *Don't Mind Me*, was published in 2008 (Chipmunkapublishing). She wrote it to help others as well as herself, and to inform mental health professionals and anyone wanting to gain an insight into mental illness. Judith contributed to *Mental Health Publishing and Empowerment* by Jason Pegler (Chipmunkapublishing, 2009), *Our Encounters with Madness* (edited by Grant, Biley & Walker, PCCS Books, 2011) and *Soul Journey* by Lisa Cherry (Wilson King Publishing, 2012). She lives by the sea with Ken and their cat Smudge. She can be contacted at www.judithhaire.com

Brendan Stone

Brendan Stone has lived with mental health problems for nearly 40 years. He lives in Sheffield and has worked extensively with users of mental health services.

Contributors

Alex

Alex is a 23-year-old, currently living in Sheffield. He graduated in 2011 with a degree in English Literature and Philosophy and now spends his time working in Sheffield, cycling around South Yorkshire and visiting family down in his home town of Shrewsbury.

Stacey Autote

Stacey Autote is a 44-year-old widow. She was raised in sunny Southern California, mostly by her single father. She obtained an Associates Degree in the Arts from El Camino College in Torrance, California, where she graduated at the top of her class and was Commencement Speaker. Stacey was also a State and National Champion Public Speaker. Wanting to reconnect with her mother, Stacey moved to extremely sunny Phoenix, Arizona. She went on to get her Bachelor's Degree from Arizona State University, where she graduated magna cum laude in Communications with a minor in Psychology and Theatre. She decided to stay in Arizona and raise a family. She has two beautiful 16-year-old daughters, Abreanna and her foster daughter April.

Catherine Carley

Some things feel like they are meant to happen. I'm not sure I believe in fate but our lives are full of coincidence and chance and it's human nature to pick up on these things. Today (Tuesday, 18 September, 2012) I finally managed to swim a mile front crawl, a major achievement for me after miles and miles of breaststroke. It's a marker of time moving on, of how we can change, of how nothing is fixed. How we tell and retell our stories evolves gradually as our memory of an event softens or hardens according to what else life chucks at us. Remember that.

I'm Catherine. I was born in Sheffield in 1968 and I still live here in 2013.

My mum was Linda. She was born in Sheffield in 1941 and died here in 2006.

Karl Davis

Karl Davis is a train driver and trade union activist, having held a number of elected positions within the train drivers' union, ASLEF and the TUC. Karl lives in Hull, East Yorkshire, and is married with a young son.

A Labour party member and community campaigner, Karl is a member of Labour's Future Candidates Programme, and has played pivotal roles in numerous local campaigns on the issues of housing, corporate manslaughter, health and safety for agency workers, and trawlermen's issues, and also acted as Secretary to the families of the crew of *FV Gaul*, a Hull-based fishing vessel lost in mysterious circumstances in the Barents Sea in 1974. Karl assisted in organising and co-ordinating the campaign to successfully pressure the government into reopening the Formal Inquiry into the vessel's loss.

Karl is a keen writer, regularly contributing articles to publications, including the *Guardian* (Comment is Free), *London Progressive Journal* and ASLEF's *Locomotive Journal*, amongst others. He has appeared on numerous local BBC News outlets connected with a multitude of issues, and engages in public speaking in support of various causes. He is currently writing his first novel, and posts on twitter as @karldavis1979. His blog can be found at www.karl-davis.blogspot.com

Tessa Glaze

I was born in the late 1950s, the youngest of three sisters. We were fortunate that my parents provided us with a stable and happy home, and in the early sixties my father was given a headship.

In August 1967 my mother left the family home, and eventually I would join her and be separated from my father and sisters. Soon afterwards I would experience the first of several anxiety-related breakdowns, which would seriously impair both my school and home life.

I got married at 18 and gave birth to two daughters, but the marriage did not last, and I became a lone parent. I met Michael soon afterwards and we spent seven years together. Suddenly in June 1987 Michael died from a fatal heart attack which caused me to plummet into despair as I struggled to keep my family going, with only my parents for support. I would eventually have a relationship with Steve, who has been my partner for the past 24 years.

After losing my stepfather, my mother was diagnosed with dementia. Her inevitable decline caused me eventually to become suicidal to the extent where I would begin to systematically plan my own death. I can be contacted at tessacheesman@yahoo.co.uk

Gilly Graham

Gilly was born in Hampshire and has two adult children. She spent 15 years working with students with special needs, many of whom were on the autistic spectrum. Gilly has co-written several Help Sheets on autism and Asperger syndrome. The Help Sheets were written for a company she previously worked for and provide information and advice for all. After reassessing her life, following the suicide of a work colleague, Gilly is following her ambition to write fiction and is currently writing her second adult fiction book as well as sending her children's stories to prospective agents and publishers.

Helen Harrop

Helen Harrop is an educational researcher, a self-taught artist, and a survivor of childhood trauma. She is in recovery from a year-long suicidal crisis that lifted completely following a short stay at the Maytree Respite Centre in 2012. Since her stay there, Helen has shared her experience of depression and suicidal thoughts on her blog, and quickly realised that telling her story gave others permission to share their stories for the first time and also provided much needed hope to fellow sufferers and their families. Helen lives with her husband and cats in York.

Chrissie Hinde

I was born in Liverpool and I have mainly grown up in England, though I spent five years living in Kenya as a child. I've been working in the Health Service as an Occupational Therapist in mental health since 1986, and am currently working in Sheffield. I've also had a small private practice in Gestalt therapy since 2000. I help to run a UK-based charity which supports a home and school set up by my mother in Kenya for children orphaned by Aids. I love gardening, art, dancing and walking in the countryside. My current passion is in Arts and Health and I'm part of a recently formed Creative Arts Steering Team (CAST) who create opportunities for mental health service-user artists in Sheffield to develop as artists and show their work.

Kathryn

I am Kathryn, half woman, half nutter, driven, with the help of Val Doonican's *Essential Hits*, by the insatiable desire to make a complete twat of myself where ever I go. Usually this entails serenading innocent males I have fleeting obsessions with. My 'modus operandi' being to find people to love in the hope it will inspire me to write. Controversially, this has proved to be a success and, once identified, the 'loved one' will not only inspire my latest work and feel truly special, but also receive personalised T-shirts, calendars, an array of non-essential items such as pens, coasters and mugs, made about them, for them. If they are truly adored then a book will be produced about the fun times we shared together, even if they have no idea what those fun times might have been. I am particularly fond of my orthopaedic consultants, Mr Blundell, Mr Kerry and Mr Davis, who clearly thought I was worth rebuilding, and as I have explained to them, you simply do not go into knee and hip arthroplasty unless you want to be truly adored.

I was a Children and Families Social Worker, which was what lured me into mentaldom at the tender age of 34, and have now come through the dark, into the light. I have written two books, *The Hoovering up of Baby Jesus* and *Cultivating MadCow*, both of which are completely bonkers and will be available to buy shortly.

Ruth Kilner

Ruth Kilner is a 26-year-old PhD student and writer. She has been a mental health service user for 15 years, having been diagnosed with borderline personality disorder (BPD) and treated for long-term major depression. She is studying for her PhD at the University of Sheffield under the supervision of Brendan Stone. The title of the PhD is 'Un-becoming the Illness: The shaping of personal over medical narratives for mental health service users through life story interviews, performed as autobiographical verbatim theatre'. She hopes, in particular, to explore the narrative of 'goodies' and 'baddies' through the symptom of 'splitting' with others diagnosed with BPD. Despite advocating for the benefits of other service users sharing their stories, Ruth has in the past been hesitant to divulge her own story as a result of the prejudice, discrimination and rejection she has faced. In this contribution, she will be reluctantly self-indulgent.

Pamela Kirk and Philippa Brook

We are a mother and daughter who survive the loss of the two other members of our immediate family to suicide. Between us, we have lost a father, a son, a husband and a brother. We are now in our eleventh year since their passing. We also live in the same house where they were found, which has been our family home for 35 years.

Lost Soul

Lost Soul was born in the City of Steel (aka Sheffield). I was adopted at the age of 6 weeks and flew the nest at the age of 16, desperate to discover the world. I worked in catering, pubs, casinos and experienced many highs and desperate lows. I was diagnosed with a personality disorder in the 1990s and contemplated suicide loads of times. As a lost soul I hope I can help others by sharing my story. If I can prevent one person from going down the downward spiral then I have achieved something special in my worthless life. I wish to dedicate this small piece of moi in ink to my soulmate, whom I shall call 'my white rose', for I was with him before the night he died. I am still awaiting the dreaded inquest. 31.5.1972 –27.3.2012.

Karen McDonald

I have lived a fulfilled life for 48 years with some amazing memories. I am a mother of two beautiful daughters who are my life. I worked as a civil servant for 22 years before changing my life and becoming a mental health nurse. I work in a psychiatric hospital in Edinburgh where I have been privileged to work with many inspirational people. I have endured sadness in my life but have escaped depression and mental health breakdown, so far! I like to think of myself as an empathic person, a good mother and friend, and most of all honest and perhaps a little too laid back. I tend not to worry about things that are out of my control. Of course these are all subjective and it would be interesting to hear what others think of me, well, perhaps one day. A good sense of humour is an important ingredient in my life too. In the past decade I have lost both my parents to illness, along with other family members, which puts life into perspective. I have also been through two serious relationship breakdowns, but what doesn't kill you makes you stronger, as they say. Choosing to share my story with you did not come easy to me. I think of

myself as a private person who likes to keep things within the family; however, after hearing so many inspirational, sometimes harrowing stories in my professional life, I have decided to share this with you today. If it helps even one person then this will make it worthwhile.
Karenmcdonald481@yahoo.co.uk

Madame de Merteuil

Born in Europe, this author has been active on the web for a very long time as 'Madame de Merteuil' or 'Marquise de Merteuil'. An historian, self-taught photoshop artist, photographer and web designer, Madame de Merteuil is also a web activist and supporter of 'We are Spartacus'.

Struggling with her mental health since childhood, Madame de Merteuil has recovered from five suicide attempts, two of which are recalled in her narrative.

She hesitated a long time before deciding to share her story due to having particularly suffered from social stigma and having been physically assaulted. She hopes coming out to a wide range of readers will help change the world of mental health for the best: diagnosed with various mental illnesses since the 1990s, Madame de Merteuil considers herself a first-hand witness to the medical and social issues surrounding mental health. She believes in a more holistic approach to recovery as well as in complete service user involvement in shaping services. She hopes to see the day when social stigma will be totally beaten. Madame de Merteuil wishes to thank those who supported her, particularly her current friends and work colleagues.

Abigal Muchecheti

Abigal Muchecheti was born in Zimbabwe. She graduated in 1999, BA in English Literature from the University of Zimbabwe, and worked in Zimbabwe and Botswana before coming to the UK for a master's degree in Business Administration at Oxford Brookes University in 2006. She worked for Oxfam and had her first book, *Married to a Devil*, published in 2012 (Chipmunkapublishing) and is working on other books. Abigal is married and lives with her husband in Faringdon and continues to write, research and blog. She can be contacted at amuchecheti05@yahoo.co.uk. Her blog is http://exquisitelady.blogspot.co.uk

Sid Prise

Sid Prise is a writer and activist born in Chicago in 1972. Sid was diagnosed with undifferentiated schizophrenia in 1997, following a prolonged mental and emotional crisis that culminated in his hearing voices, which he deals with to this day. He has been writing seriously since 1994, and published his first novel, *True Faith*, in 2003. His essay 'An Ethics of Sanity', and two novels, *The Wobbly* and *It Will Not Last the Night*, have been published with Chipmunka Publishing in the UK. He has recently self-published *Chameleon's Morrow*, the first in a series of fantasy novels called 'Twilight of the Gods', available at lulu.com. More of his writings can be found at his website, smallaxebooks.com. Sid writes about living with madness in a mad society. His work represents one mad person's attempt to make sense of his personal narrative within the greater narrative of world civilization, and to create a better, healthier narrative, both for civilization and for himself. He resides with his partner, Kathy, and their friends in a collective house in Chicago.

Jo Rhodes

My name is Jo Rhodes and I was married to Adam Rhodes for seven-and-a-half years, from 1999 to 2007. We lived in Bodmin in Cornwall for much of that time, surrounded by both our families and friends. We shared a love of animals, comedy, music and *The West Wing* and I supported his support of Tottenham Football Club!

During our marriage, I miscarried twice and was pregnant for a third time when my husband took his own life. Since his untimely passing, I have given birth to a little girl who is beautiful and wonderful as well as being my own miracle. Being a mother has given me a whole new perspective on life and being widowed in my twenties has given me a whole new perspective on death. Both events have led me to discover a new faith and also a new trust in humankind. I love walking the many moorland and coastal paths that are so abundant here in the south-west with my daughter and our sprollie dog, even if it is raining! I try to make the most of every day; life is too precious not to.

Neil Ritchie

I'm 43 and I live in Portlethen, just outside Aberdeen in Scotland. I'm a working parent of two children, one of whom is autistic, the other in the process of being assessed for ADHD. I'm actively trying to raise awareness of autistic spectrum disorders. I am currently working in the public sector after gaining a degree in Business Studies at Robert Gordon University in Aberdeen. Suicide affected me directly in 2003 when my closest friend took his own life aged 35 following a long struggle with manic depression, giving me new insight and understanding of suicide and a desire to raise awareness of a taboo subject.
neileritchie@claymore33.plus.com

Kathryn Rosenfeld

Kathryn Rosenfeld grew up in New York City, where she was born in 1971. She received a BA from Antioch College in Yellow Springs, Ohio and an MA from the University of Cincinnati. She was assistant editor of the late *New Art Examiner.* Her various occupations have also included pre-school teacher, freelance arts journalist, and bicycle mechanic. She has lived in Chicago since 1999, where today she raises vegetables and chickens with her partner, Sid Prise, and their many housemates and cats.

Dolly Sen

Born in London in 1970, Dolly Sen is a writer, director, artist, film-maker, poet, performer, playwright, mental health consultant, music-maker and public speaker. Since her much-acclaimed book, *The World is Full of Laughter*, was published by Chipmunka in 2002, she has had five further books published, had a succession of performance roles around Europe, directed several plays and films, appeared on TV, and has worked at City Hall in London and Oxford University. She has exhibited her art in the UK, France and the Netherlands.

This is staggering since she dropped out of school at 14 and has no formal qualifications. She has also had to share her life with severe mental health difficulties. She was told she would never amount to anything but would end up in jail or Broadmoor, and she believed this and was on her way there when she changed her belief into the one of believing she could do anything she wanted to do.

This proves that the mind is an amazing thing; it can drive you mad and inspire you in the same breath. And that you can do anything if you believe you can do it.

www.dollysen.com

dollysen70@hotmail.com

Michael Skinner

Michael Skinner is a nationally known, award-winning advocate survivor addressing the issues of trauma, abuse and mental health concerns through public speaking and his music – he has spoken at the National Press Club, was a keynote presenter for a conference held by the United Nations, the State Department and Georgetown University on the sexual exploitation and trafficking of children and adults, and he has appeared on many TV, radio and Internet shows (he was part of the Oprah Winfrey shows that addressed the issues of males sexually abused as children). His music and advocacy website has been visited by well over a million

visitors and he has formed the non-profit, The Surviving Spirit, which offers hope, healing and help for those impacted by trauma, abuse and mental health concerns through the creative arts, advocacy, education, a monthly newsletter and website.
www.mskinnermusic.com
www.survivingspirit.com
mikeskinner@comcast.net
mike.skinner@survivingspirit.com

Georgina Smith
Georgina Smith is a Service User Governor in her local Health and Social Care Trust. She has been bipolar for 37 years and currently trains others in various aspects of mental health.

Felicity Stennett
In November 2012 Felicity sadly died due to a massive blood clot in her heart, leaving her husband of 5 months and her 8-year-old son. Below is the biography she wrote for inclusion in this book.

Felicity is a 24-year-old whose main priority in life is her son and husband. She used to be outgoing and successful. She enjoyed caring for abandoned kittens, long walks with the dog, spending time with her son: playing games and teaching him things. She was doing her midwifery training in Sheffield with the intention of doing a master's degree, getting a house and supporting her little family. Her first psychiatric admission took place when she was 21. She felt as if her life had stopped and she had distanced herself from all her friends. Her career was ruined, whilst her self-worth and confidence came crashing down along with her desire to live. She was frightened of exploring issues with the nurses. Frightened what would happen if they knew she had been sexually abused as a child. Frightened of their response.

Felicity has had many suicide attempts but chose to write about this one as it is the closest she got to death. She is now diagnosed with emotionally unstable personality disorder, also known as borderline personality disorder.

Her self-harming has resulted in the need for 31 units of blood. She has had 12 psychiatric admissions including admissions to High Intensity wards. Although she fantasises about living a normal, functional life, she continues to struggle with her mental health and finds it difficult to imagine a future other than on a psychiatric ward.

Jayne Stewart

My brother killed himself in 1999. Since then I have often asked myself why I am alive when he is dead, and this question has led me to engage in an ongoing exploration of the process of living and dying and to a conscious process of deciding what in my life wants to live more and what needs to die in order for this new life to flourish.

For the last 12 years I have been researching suicidal processes informed by my own life experience and Arnold Mindell's Process Oriented Psychology. Using the wisdom distilled from this research I now run Suicidal Wisdom workshops for counsellors and therapists and for people directly affected by suicide, either through bereavement, or through having their own suicidal thoughts and feelings.

I have been a teacher most of my working life, beginning with mathematics and including IT and English as a Second Language. I currently teach a creative, spiritual and therapeutic dance practice.

Recently I moved to live by the sea in order to write a book about my experiences called *Eat the Poison and Survive*. I am married and have a grown-up son.

Cath Walsh

I am a 33-year-old wife and mother of two and, when not on maternity leave, work as a children's yoga teacher and Reiki practitioner, having initially qualified as a primary school teacher in 2002.

My younger sister committed suicide in 2007, age 25, after suffering a lifetime of anxiety, depression and eventual diagnosis of a borderline personality disorder.

I was part of a SOBS (Sharers of Bereavement by Suicide) support group and got involved with the bereavement centre we ran for a year. I am making sense of my loss by helping other people, sharing what I have been through with others, and helping them find ways to move forward. Suicide bereavement can impact so greatly on the lives of the loved ones left behind, and there needs to be more support and under-standing of that.

I also hope that with the Reiki and yoga teaching I can help people who have suffered great loss too. Both yoga and other holistic treatments helped me begin to regain my sense of self outside of the bereavement and move forward to living with the loss, and I hope that I can help others as I have been helped.

Dawn Willis

Dawn Willis was born in Newcastle upon Tyne. She joined Northumbria Police Force after sixth form. Following the births of her first two children she became unwell with postpartum psychosis. Treatment was successful and she went on to re-marry and raise her three children whilst working as a Private Investigator. Following several periods of major depressive illness it was discovered that Dawn had been living with bipolar disorder since the onset of adolescence. Interested in understanding the nature of the illness, she studied and has since worked in support roles in both Rethink Mental Illness and Mind. She has co-authored two reports: 'How to support peer support: Evaluating the first steps in a healthcare community', *Journal of Public Mental Health*, 2010, and *Responsible Reform: A Report on the Proposed Changes to Disability Living Allowance* (Spartacus Report), 2012.

Determined to raise awareness around stigma and discrimination she is an active social media campaigner, blogger, public speaker and independent trainer. Her achievements in this field have been recognised. In 2010 she won the Rethink Mental Illness 'Pringle Award' and was a finalist in Mind Media Awards 2011.

She lives in Devon and enjoys writing poetry and painting. Her website can be found at https://dawnwillis.wordpress.com

References

Barnes, J (2011) *The Sense of an Ending*. London: Jonathan Cape (Kindle edition).

Church, K (1995) *Forbidden Narratives: Critical autobiography as social science*. London and New York: Routledge.

Grant, A (2011a) Introduction: Learning from narrative accounts of the experience of mental health challenges. In A Grant, F Biley & H Walker (Eds) *Our Encounters with Madness* (pp. 1–10). Ross-on-Wye: PCCS Books.

Grant, A (2011b) Performing the room: Four days on an acute ward. In A Grant, F Biley & H Walker (Eds) *Our Encounters with Madness* (pp. 125–30). Ross-on-Wye: PCCS Books.

Grant, A, Biley, F & Walker, H (Eds) (2011) *Our Encounters with Madness*. Ross-on-Wye: PCCS Books.

Grant, A & Zeeman, L (2012) Whose story is it? An autoethnography concerning narrative identity. *The Qualitative Report, 17*(72), 1–12.

Kafka, F (1925/1953) *The Trial*. Harmondsworth: Penguin.

Lakoff, G & Johnson, M (2003) *Metaphors We Live By*. Chicago and London: University of Chicago Press.

Marsh, I (2010) *Suicide: Foucault, history and truth*. Cambridge: Cambridge University Press.

Richardson, L (1997) *Fields of Play: Constructing an academic life*. New Brunswick, NJ: Rutgers University Press.

Schon, DA (1987) *Educating the Reflective Practitioner: Toward a new design for teaching and learning in the professions*. San Francisco: Jossey-Bass.

wikipedia.org/wiki/Arthur_Koestler [accessed 12 February 2013]

Our Encounters with Madness

Alec Grant, Fran Biley and
Hannah Walker (eds)
ISBN 978 1 906254 38 4 (2011)
rrp £18.00, website £17.00

A collection of user, carer and survivor narratives, this book is grouped under five themes: On diagnosis; Stories of experience; Experiencing the system; On being a carer; Abuse and survival.

The book will be of great benefit to students of mental health and narrative inquiry, users and carers, and to those generally interested in the pedagogy of suffering. Unlike most other books in this genre, the narratives are unmediated. Written by experts by experience, there are no professional biomedical or psychotherapeutic commentaries, which often serve to capture and tame, or sanitise, such stories of direct experience.

Our Encounters with Self-Harm

Charley Baker, Fran Biley and
Clare Shaw (eds)
ISBN 978 1 906254 63 6 (2013)
rrp £18.00, website £17.00

Too often, our understanding of the unique and complex experiences of people who self-harm is limited to concepts of mental illness, disorder and disease. Yet these stories demonstrate the strength, survival and recovery of people with rich and diverse lives.

Inspiring, hopeful and at times challenging to read, this book will promote understanding and compassion, and improve attitudes towards those who are encountering self-harm.

Thinking About Suicide: Contemplating and comprehending the urge to die

David Webb
ISBN 978 1 906254 28 5 (2010)
rrp £14.00, website £13.00

The literature of suicidology has studiously ignored the voice of those who actually experience suicidal feelings. David Webb suggests this is no accidental oversight but a very deliberate and systematic exclusion of this critically important first-person knowledge. The only thing that is banished with even more vigour from suicidology is mention of the spiritual wisdom that set the author free of his persistent urge to die.

Webb rejects the dominant medical model that claims suicide is caused by some notional mental illness. *Thinking About Suicide* calls for broad community conversation on suicide that is required to bring it out of the closet as a public health issue.